The essence of Campaigning Fundraising in 52 exhibits and 199 web links

WHAT DO YOU MEAN, CAMPAIGNING FUNDRAISING?

Voluntary action funded by individuals sits deep at the core of our civilisation. It's our society's tangible, practical, freely given expression of concern and support for its weaker, more vulnerable members. Most of our society's great causes got started because concerned people came together to raise money to change something that urgently needed changing, or to save something that very much deserved saving. Their impact on the character and development of our society cannot be over-estimated. And their continued existence and effectiveness depends upon successful fundraising.

Fundraising is a powerful catalyst for change, but it shouldn't ever be separated from the cause you're raising money for. People don't give for things to stay the same. Always, they give to make a difference, to bring about a positive shift, even transformation. So, by referring to this activity merely as fundraising, simply emphasising the money, we made a basic big mistake, a mistake we've paid dearly for and are still paying for, so should rectify once and for all. Campaigning fundraising it has to be, for the fundraiser's job is to directly, delightfully connect each and every donor with the difference he or she is making. That, in essence, is what campaigning fundraising is for. It's why, when done properly, this can be the very best job going.

The White Lion Press

OTHER BOOKS BY THIS AUTHOR

Storytelling can change the world, The White Lion Press, London, softback, 2014.

The Field by the River, Anova Books, London, hardback, 2008, softback, 2009, and Kindle, 2013.

The Zen of Fundraising, Jossey-Bass, San Francisco, softback, 2006.

Tiny Essentials of an Effective Volunteer Board, The White Lion Press, London, softback, 2004.

Relationship Fundraising, second edition, Jossey-Bass, San Francisco, hardback 2002. The White Lion Press, London, hardback, 1992.

Friends for Life, The White Lion Press, London, hardback, 1996.

How to Produce Inspiring Annual Reports, Directory of Social Change, London, softback, 2000, with Karin Weatherup.

Website and blog, www.kenburnett.com

The essence of

Campaigning Fundraising

in 52 exhibits and 199 web links

Ken Burnett

Foreword by Roger M. Craver

Published in association with the SOFII Foundation, UK and *The Agitator*, USA.

The Agitator

sofii showcase of fundraising innovation and inspiration

The White Lion Press

The White Lion Press, London. www.whitelionpress.com

ISBN: 978-0-9553993-7-4

The SOFII Foundation is a charity registered in the UK no. 1124743 and a company limited by guarantee, company registered no. 06530274.
www.sofii.org

First printed 2021

British Library Cataloguing-in-Publication Data.
A catalogue record for this book is available from the British Library.

Cover illustration by Roy Williams.
Design and print production by Bradbury and Williams.
Printed and bound in the United Kingdom by CPI Group (UK) Ltd, Croydon CR0 4YY

Disclaimer
For a variety of reasons outside the publisher's control, web links can change and a once-valid link can suddenly stop working. At the time of going to press all of the links in this book were checked and were working. While we can ensure that links to the SOFII site are kept up-to-date, we don't have control over links to other sites. Should you find a link that isn't working as it should, please let us know by emailing joe@sofii.org. Alternatively, please go to www.sofii.org where all of the book's links will be found, as current as we can make them. We apologise for any inconvenience.

All views expressed here are those of the author and do not necessarily reflect the views of either The SOFII Foundation or *The Agitator*.

IN MEMORY OF MARIE BURNETT

co-founder and editor-in-chief of SOFII.org,
The Showcase of Fundraising Innovation and Inspiration.

Alongside our generous co-collaborators on *The Agitator*, this book is dedicated to the SOFII workers, Carolina Herrera, Joanna Culling and Joe Burnett; also to trustees of the SOFII Foundation, Fiona Duncan, David Carrington (Hon secretary, treasurer and former trustee), Meredith Niles, Craig Linton and Richard Turner; to newly appointed trustees (for their evident potential) Rachel Moore, Angélique Masse Nguyen, Charmaine Shah, Andrew Watt and Heather Little and to all the legions of supporters, donors, volunteers and users who make SOFII possible by freely contributing and sharing priceless inspirational content that will change the world.

What others have said about *The essence of Campaigning Fundraising*

'This book does not deserve a place on your shelf. It deserves to be open on your desk in a place of practical use, as a campaigning fundraiser who wants to do and be better: dog-eared, marked-up, pages flagged for future world-changing projects. The links and exhibits contained here transformed the way I do my work as a fundraising copywriter (and continue to do so). May they likewise transform the work you do to make this world a better place by giving your donors the chance to be the generous, compassionate, caring people they are – as deeply committed as you are to making this world a better place for us all. Use this book daily. I know I will.'

Lisa Sargent, campaigning fundraising copywriter, USA

'Thirty years ago, Ken Burnett rescued donors by putting them in the centre. In this new book, Ken rescues fundraisers by showing them they are campaigners. They don't raise funds. They work with donors yearning to make their world more just, more educated, more healthy, greener. Precious donors who, guided by campaigning fundraisers, want to be inspired, angered, impassioned and given a chance to be heroes. This book, filled with powerful examples accompanied by Ken's sharp wit and profound insights, is a treasure.'

David Love, author and leading environmental campaigning fundraiser, Canada

'If you raise money for a cause you believe in – whether you're a volunteer or a professional – this book will pay for itself the first day you look at it. *The essence of Campaigning Fundraising* is filled with great advice from author Ken Burnett, as well as wisdom from dozens of successful and ground-breaking direct response campaigns archived on SOFII.'

Nick Allen, digital fundraiser for UNICEF, Amnesty and many more, USA

'This book is very timely post-Covid pandemic, as need for raising money has increased tremendously and fundraisers are not only expected to be good at what they do but to be great at what they do. This is what Ken teaches us in this book; he takes us on the journey to become a great fundraiser through learning the history of great fundraising. The more we know about the great fundraising of the past, the better prepared we are to make the great fundraising of the future.'

Ikhlaq Hussain, lecturer, trainer, head of philanthropy and partnerships, Orphans In Need, UK

'Through the years Ken's words have launched a thousand fundraising careers. His latest collection of words – *Campaigning Fundraising* – will inspire a thousand more to join in the crusade to change our world. SOFII.org is part historical record, part labour of love and part treasure chest of fundraising riches. This book will take you, the reader, through SOFII's vast exhibit hall – where you will get a closer look at the beautiful details that lie within. Lovingly crafted by a true master, this book should sit on the corner of every enlightened fundraiser's desk.'

John Lepp, partner, Agents of Good, Canada

'When Ken Burnett writes, I listen. This is the book I wish I had when I left university to work in the for-change sector. A masterful distillation of time-tested principles and nuts-and-bolts wisdom that only comes from hard-earned experience. It is a map, a compass, and a North Star that can guide you through the body of work in fundraising so you, too, can experience the kind of exciting, successful, and rewarding career the social change sector is uniquely positioned to offer. A brilliant gift for any graduate as well as seasoned professional who wants to change the world.'

Dr Julie Berthoud-Jury, international fundraising consultant, Switzerland

'This is a fantastic book. Chock full of inspiring stories, well-told, and ones that will help you to raise a lot of money. Once again Ken Burnett has given all of us a gift that will help the profession, and most importantly, promote the social progress we all desire.'

Harvey McKinnon, author and president, Harvey McKinnon Associates, Vancouver, Canada

"The truth told well' is a phrase frequently used by Ken Burnett to inspire fundraisers. *The essence of Campaigning Fundraising* is just that, *the truth told well*. Cleverly written and highly readable, this book is a brilliant reminder to all world changers and leaders about the IMPACT we can all make, if we do it well. You can hear the calming, considered voice of Ken on every page. A must-read for everyone in the sector or thinking of joining it.'

Michelle Berriman, executive director, Fundraising Institute of New Zealand

'Thank you for writing it. We need it and the repositioning of fundraising is welcome. I think many fundraisers (young and old) will like to describe themselves as campaigning fundraisers. It should hit home.'

Mark Phillips, managing director, Bluefrog Fundraising, London, UK

'I love this book, I love its spirit and I think the fundraising sector will love it too. The descriptor campaigning fundraising captures the work of fundraisers eloquently and accurately. The book and its exhibits will be very encouraging for those looking to join the sector, equipping them to take a donor-focused approach and tell their supporters the right stories in the right way at the right time.'

Ryan Burdock, associate director – fundraising, Prospectus, London, UK

Contents

A glaring need for re-focusing
Foreword, by Roger M. Craver, *The Agitator*

The crying need for fundraisers and fundraising leaders to re-examine what we do and how we do it has now taken on an existential urgency.

Democracy is under threat. Truth, the essence of any free and democratic society, is in decay, assaulted by forces intent on imposing a frightening and conspiratorial alternate reality. Trust in governments, leaders, the press, non-profits and even among citizens themselves is at an all-time low. For good measure a global pandemic now tops this heap of woe.

Fortunately, in troubling times like these ordinary people and the organizations they band together to create have historically proven amazingly resilient: capable of rescue, restoration and renewal.

In my 55 years of organizing and campaigning for change I've witnessed first-hand the power of organized, ordinary folks. Name an issue where there's a problem and you're likely to find a group of caring people banded together in support of a solution. Women's suffrage. Hunger. Homelessness. Human Rights. Civil Rights. Animal Rights. Conservation. Peace. Climate Change. Whatever the issue there are scores of non-profit household names tackling the problem.

Nearly every one of these organizations requires a multitude of committed activists and donors to fuel the change it seeks. And that means *fundraising and fundraisers.*

Given the high stakes now at play for the future we will not only need more fundraisers, but better fundraisers. A lot more. A lot better.

To address the challenges we face not only must we acknowledge our sector's crumbling infrastructure of lower and lower retention rates, fewer and fewer donors, and more and more organizations chasing a shrinking base of trust and support. Equally we must admit we're failing to properly recruit and adequately train and inspire a new generation of fundraisers. *We must do something about all this. We must change.*

Right here – in your hands – you hold a precious guide to how we might change. You'll discover that we don't have to start over and build from scratch. Rather, we do have to look at first principles and challenge virtually every assumption we've taken for granted for far too long.

Fortunately, Ken Burnett, with this new book, is back in his role as master guide. Just as he did 30 years ago with his revolutionary *Relationship Fundraising: a donor-based approach to the business of raising money,* he now delivers a wealth of advice and advice-by-classic examples that should give every fundraiser a big, big nudge.

Even if our acquisition, retention and development results were miles better than they actually are, there still would be a glaring need for a re-focusing – exactly the aim of this book.

Whether novice or veteran these pages contain a treasure trove of value for every fundraiser:

* For the young would-be fundraiser – and there are plenty of them – how do they cut through the clutter of blogs, books and conferences to find what really matters, for them? And should they even be calling themselves fundraisers, in the first place?
* Fundraising leaders need a motivational and informed kick in the pants too. If you had just a few hours to brief a new recruit to your fundraising or campaigning departments, what are the top 20, or even top 100, key things you'd want them to really know and master?

The strength of this book is in the cumulative evidence it provides for a very specific, clearly articulated philosophy of how to do campaigning fundraising and donor retention and relationship development in the early years of the 21st century and beyond.

Through 52 exhibits and 199 web links it shows where we've got things wrong and how we can massively improve and thus multiply our voluntary sector's impact on the problems we seek to solve and the benefits we bring to our society.

Like an archaeologist uncovering and highlighting great riches from the past, the author taps into the motherlode of fundraising riches available 24/7 online–The Showcase of Fundraising Innovation and Inspiration (SOFII.org). Ken Burnett helped found SOFII in 2007, and it's been growing ever since. SOFII is a working wonder. A carefully curated repository of hundreds of examples of the best campaigns and thousands of articles offering professional fundraisers the best available guidance and support. Fortunately for the reader, the examples cited in this book conveniently contain links and QR codes back to the original entries on SOFII and a few too on *The Agitator*. Link. See. Admire. Think.

Importantly, the book's title deserves special note. "*Campaigning*

Fundraising" doesn't flow easily off the tongue, but it's the absolutely accurate descriptor of a function so essential to creating a better world.

As you'll see in the example-packed pages of this book *campaigning fundraising* is unique, complex and quirky. Way too many people too often assume it's simple, easy, merely a matter of asking people to give the money. And if ever more and more money is needed (which it always is) too many fundraisers and others have assumed they just have to ask more people, more often, more vigorously, for bigger sums. (Perhaps this explains why people instinctively cross the street to avoid a fundraiser, and why at parties any campaigning fundraiser incautious enough to announce what she or he does for a living can, in an instant, effectively clear a room.)

Fundraising is not popular. Neither is it well understood nor appreciated. This book should change that. Campaigning fundraisers and what they do should have very much higher status and respect in our society because of both the good they make possible and the benefits they bring. Fundraising enables social impact and empowers communities, so leads to dynamic and lasting social change.

Our society would be much less healthy and self-sustaining without campaigning fundraisers. Their work cannot be entirely delegated to the state nor reassigned to commercial suppliers. A thriving fundraising and campaigning community enables a vibrant, thriving third sector – the voluntary, not-for-profit or for-change sector – which in turn ensures a stable, balanced and caring society that provides ample means for all its constituents to share in its obligations and duties, to care for and share with those less fortunate than themselves and to otherwise improve our world.

Campaigning fundraisers can and must go further and aim higher. This book sets out a road map and a timeline for improving and accelerating a vital function that's needed more now than ever.

Roger M. Craver, Editor
The Agitator
Chilmark, Massachusetts

Roger Craver's Wikipedia entry describes him as an American author, fundraiser and campaigner for liberal political and progressive causes. Roger was among the first to apply direct mail methodology to movement and political fundraising. He has said that the frustration and alienation that Americans felt during the 1960s developed a social environment that encouraged the success of the fundraising method. Later scholars would call Craver an early pioneer for democratic and progressive direct mail efforts. In 1969 he cofounded Common Cause and then went on to found Craver, Mathews, Smith & Company, the consulting firm that helped launch the National Organization for Women (NOW), the National Abortion Rights Action League (NARAL) the National Council to Control Handguns and to grow the American Civil Liberties Union (ACLU), Planned Parenthood, Sierra Club, Amnesty International, Greenpeace, the Southern Poverty Law Center, and help dozens more non-profits such as Habitat for Humanity and Heifer International gain traction through direct mail fundraising. A leading opinion-former in the non-profit sector worldwide, Roger is now editor of the influential *Agitator*.

www.agitator.thedonorvoice.com

Introduction
What campaigning fundraising is really about

> **'What drives great fundraising is value. We create value, and money follows value. A perhaps more poetic way to say this is that we make donors' dreams come true. So, every time you read the word "fundraising"...please think "creating value".'**
>
> David Love, *Green Green*, 2020

IT'S ABOUT MUCH MORE THAN THE MONEY

Effective campaigning fundraising isn't just about what raises most money, far from it. Donors' gifts drive societal changes that shape our communities. Events spread campaign messages, bringing people together to make good things happen and build social cohesion. Trusts and foundations exist solely to give away money to the most deserving of causes, money often made in less socially useful activities. Major donors find in charities an acceptable way to share their surplus wealth, in the process getting to feel good about the differences they make. In exchange for an easily affordable slice of their disposable funds, less well-heeled individuals can also share the warm glow of giving and enjoy a sense of achievement too. Charity shops provide bargains for everyone and are lifesavers for society's most vulnerable, recycling quality used goods to people who often desperately need low-cost essentials. Companies use charities to build their employees' morale, sense of self-worth and social purpose. Face-to-face fundraising introduces tens of thousands of young people each year to caring for good causes, who in turn go on to recruit generally younger-than-usual donors. And much more. The capital donors bring is as much emotional as transactional. Most of our society's great causes got started because concerned people came together to raise money to change something that urgently needed changing, or to save something that very much deserved saving. Their impact on the character and development of our society cannot be over-estimated.

WHY ADD 'CAMPAIGNING' BEFORE 'FUNDRAISING'?

I like David Love's notion that when we say the word 'fundraising' we should think more broadly. Sadly, people don't, they think it means simply asking for money. So, we need to add something. This project started out as a book about fundraising, but even a short way in I realised that to be accurate, it had to broaden its scope. We need to move beyond the merely monetary aspect of what fundraisers do, to link their activities to the change that a donor's money brings. As if to emphasise that, in fundraising, asking for money is the last thing that you should do, fundraising invariably goes hand in hand with campaigning, though always the campaigning has to come first. Whether it's eradicating cancer, tackling climate change or providing access to education and excellence for aspiring young musicians, you can't remove the campaigning element from fundraising. Otherwise, it's just asking people for money, for no evident benefit or good reason. People don't give for things to remain as they are – they give to see change, always. So campaigning fundraising it has to be. Many of our sector's recent, most dangerous, most enduring problems stem from fundraisers focusing on asking bluntly for money rather than on answering what's uppermost in every donor's priorities, which is, 'How can I help?', 'Will my help make a difference?', and 'Will my help get through?' Campaigning fundraising is about helping people to understand, savour and enjoy the end result as much as it is about helping them to get there.

Your organisation is a truck, donors' money is its fuel and cargo. Its sole purpose is to take the supporter's contribution and the difference that makes directly and promptly to where it's needed. So, you can't separate the mission from the money or from the supporter experience. Without the former and the latter, the bit in the middle won't come or won't last. Simple. Fundraisers can show that, through campaigning fundraising, small change can make a big difference. But in coming up with a name for this activity it might have been wiser had fundraisers emphasised the difference the money can make at least as much as emphasising the money they want. Donors and their causes enjoy a strong, mutually beneficial relationship. Fundraising above all is about the change charities and their supporters want to see in this world. So, by referring to this activity merely as fundraising we made a basic big mistake, a mistake we've paid dearly for and are still paying for, so should rectify once and for all. Campaigning fundraising it has to be, for the fundraiser's job is to directly and delightfully connect the donor with the difference he or she is making. That, in essence, is what campaigning fundraising is all about.

'First open their hearts and minds. Their wallets will follow.'

Harold Sumption, founder, the International Fundraising Congress, Holland

> **'Fundraising is the most important source of income for voluntary bodies and giving by individuals is the most important area in fundraising.'**
>
> *The Status of UK Fundraising 2018 Benchmark Report*, Blackbaud Europe

> **'The market for something to believe in is infinite.'**
>
> Hugh MacLeod, @thegapingvoid, using art to transform business

Voluntary action funded by individuals sits deep at the core of our civilisation. It's our society's tangible, practical, freely given expression of concern and support for its weaker, more vulnerable members. While we might argue whether the State should do more or less for society's most needy and vulnerable, no one wants the State to do everything. Of course, all organisations campaigning for social change need to work closely and harmoniously with the government of the day, but fundamental to the quality and effectiveness of the relationship is the capacity of voluntary organisations to retain their independence. Inevitably, that independence comes from successful fundraising. The often remote, at times stifling hand of any central government system can dull creativity, flexibility and passion, all essential for appropriate and effective service provision. Over-reliance on central government to tackle all social ills and needs would also deny ordinary individuals the chance to direct their own giving and to delight in and benefit from the achievements their giving makes possible. The independent voluntary sector exists to fill the gaps in state provision and also to lead the way in doing things better. The fuel for all its actions comes from fundraising. Thriving voluntary sector causes are a barometer of society's health and effective functioning. To stretch the metaphor, they work best as a nippy little Nissan Micra rather than a huge gas-guzzling Chevrolet. So, as fundraising fuels all this great work, its role in all our lives is hugely important.

Fundraising is communication. It's the inspiration business and it's the truth, told well. Fundraising for good causes is all about winning hearts and minds first, so that wallets, purses, pocketbooks and electronic funds transfers happily follow later, to stimulate and generate significant change. Money is the means to that end but it's never the end itself, so fundraising, campaigning and the communication of inspiration are all inextricably intertwined.

> **'Raising money for a cause is a unique business area. It benefits from many of the highest human emotions and is lucky enough not to be burdened by some of the basest. One thing is certain – a fundraising transaction is fundamentally different from a commercial business transaction. Although fundraisers have much to learn from commercial practice they will commit a fatal, suicidal error if they embrace commercial practices too enthusiastically.'**
>
> Ken Burnett, *Relationship Fundraising*, 1992

In that nearly 30-year-old book I went on to suggest that rather than focusing on the money, fundraisers should first focus on the people sending it. I stressed the importance of understanding donors and delivering what donors want, then explained how to do that, in elaborate detail. Increasingly over the years the simple truth that forms the core of that and all my subsequent books on this subject has become ever clearer to me and to many others too, though sadly, not to all. Had this truth been universally acknowledged the UK's fundraising community couldn't possibly have suffered the sustained, near catastrophic criticism that so damagingly afflicted our sector in 2015 and beyond as print and broadcast media persistently catalogued in lurid, heart-rending detail systematic, inappropriate, even aggressive fundraising practices from charities (see exhibits 13 and 22 in this book). Fortuitously, that near catastrophe has become a catalyst for change – providing we can grasp it firmly and keep our nerve and our commitment to delivering a great donor experience. That change seems likely to lead soon if not imminently to what's been called a new era of responsible fundraising. Rather obviously, inspiring and delivering a consistently excellent supporter experience is what fundraising should be all about.

> **'If giving is a good experience, donors will do more of it. If it isn't, they'll soon stop.'**
>
> *The 6Ps* summary document of the Commission on the Donor Experience, 2016

The logical and emotional case for this is, thankfully, delightfully simple: if we do right by our donors, they'll do right by us. That said, fundraising is remarkably resilient. Since 2017 the sector has bounced back from a PR nightmare that would have sunk most other industries. Though, I submit, there's still some way to go. Others more qualified than I am will come up with explanations for this seeming recovery but to me it seems obvious that while donors may dislike the way some fundraisers go about the business of asking, they won't want the innocent beneficiaries to suffer for the inappropriate actions of the fundraisers. While bad fundraising persists, many donors will give in spite of the fundraisers, perhaps as much as because of them.

We must change that.

We fundraisers offer no tangible good or service that our customers have to have. If giving is a good experience, donors will do more of it. If it isn't, they'll soon stop. Yet we also have potentially the greatest proposition of all for would-be world-changers – we offer people of goodwill the chance, the potential, the possibility, even the certainty of making a difference in a troubled world. And we can prove it. We can offer donors sound assurance of impact that will show them that their gift has been the difference they want to see. As such, fundraisers are catalysts of change. More than that, if we deploy our creativity, passion, wit and wisdom wisely we can deliver, consistently, a fulfilling, richly rewarding supporter experience that will play a constructive part in adding purpose, meaning and achievement into our supporters' busy lives, which will inspire donors to involve their family, friends and contacts so we can engage far more donors than we do at present. And there's more. As we'll see later, giving is actually good for you, your health, your marriage, your physical and mental well-being.[1]
The propositions we need to make shouldn't be too hard to sell.

A CORNUCOPIA OF TREASURES

Promoting social improvement offers unsurpassed career opportunities. More than anything, young people coming into the world of work want to do something worthwhile with their life that will make a difference, maybe even change the world. Campaigning fundraising allows them to do that and much more. Indeed, some will find it a vocation. So campaigning fundraising should find a prominent place in every school's careers department.

Consistently down the ages some of our world's most creative minds have bent their talents, passion and experience to the task of communicating to stir and shape the mutually beneficial relationship

1 Dr Tara Swart, *The Future of Giving is Smarter Giving*, Barclays Private Bank, 2019.

fundraisers share with donors. In doing so they've bequeathed a staggeringly rich body of work to us that has formed and shaped and will continue to influence our fundraising and campaigning output long into the future. The work that forms the chronicles of fundraising is scintillating, vast and complex, as are the lessons that can be learned from it. In 2007 my late wife Marie and I decided to set up a website – SOFII.org, The Showcase of Fundraising Innovation and Inspiration. Our purpose was to capture and make available the best of this content, for free and permanently, for the benefit of campaigning fundraising change-makers everywhere. Within SOFII.org the campaigning fundraising communications tyro will find literally hundreds of the world's best and most instructive illustrated case histories of effective fundraising practice, plus more than 1,000 opinion and 'how to' articles, all carefully documented, clearly presented, free and available online 24/7. Do check out SOFII.org and register also for their free weekly updates that list newly added content to this growing body of practical, useful knowledge and insights, plus remind you of treasures worth revisiting and upcoming events that you won't want to miss.

> **'Fundraising's history is, in essence, a history of big, bold ideas shared widely and borrowed wisely.'**
>
> From a letter inviting contributions to start the SOFII website, 2007

ABOUT THIS BOOK

As a young fundraiser in the late 1970s I thought – in my then boundless ignorance of my chosen career – that I and my generation were the front line, the pioneers of fundraising, that I and my peers had discovered the wonders of donor recruitment, off-the-page advertising, had introduced telephone fundraising, street fundraising, inserts, door-to-door, direct mail and much more besides. How foolish I was! The truth is dramatically and very helpfully different, as the following 52 exhibits and their multiple links will show. For there's a rich, diverse, very international body of work that constantly shines light on the endeavours of all the world's fundraisers and has done since the earliest recorded times. This body of work has the capacity to do more good in this world than anything else I know.

Though inevitably mere abridged indicators from this vast treasure trove of accumulated knowledge the 52 exhibits showcased in this book collectively present a hopefully irresistible vision of what campaigning fundraising could be and should be – the essence of the art and craft of securing, shaping and developing relationships with our donors. In other words, the business of inspiring others to take action to make a difference that will make life better for all. For the purposes of this book an exhibit here can be a single artefact or several that are connected; it can be a way of doing things, a concept or an aspect of improving practice, even an era from history. Sometimes articles or case histories or both can be linked together under a common theme. While the term is flexible, what's covered in each exhibit is always significant and worth exploring further.

While this book, *The essence of Campaigning Fundraising in 52 exhibits and 199 web links*, is complete and entire of itself, you'll gain lots more if you click on to or paste into your browser (scan the QR codes as a shortcut) the 199 web links in the title and follow where they lead. For good measure we've added in a raft of links to content from our friends across the Atlantic, *The Agitator*. Follow these to find an additional, often different take on the issues these exhibits raise. All of this book's links are listed at the end of each exhibit and can be accessed using the USB key that comes with this book or, if that's missing, they can be readily found online from the home page of SOFII.org. Knowledge is a gateway to all sorts of riches and opportunities so the purpose of this book, quite simply, is to show you what you need, where to go to find it and how to get there in the shortest possible time.

I WISH I'D THOUGHT OF THAT!

If you're looking for big ideas to change the world you've come to the right place. And you can even tell the rest of the world about the best of it. There's so much inspiration and innovation around in this extraordinary business sector that the SOFII Foundation has been able to run a series of spectacularly successful events in various countries around the globe. These feature seven-minute summaries of the lessons we can learn from studying and even borrowing individual ideas and successful campaigning fundraising achievements, each idea presented by a fundraiser who admires it. In just seven minutes or less a succession of volunteer speakers are given the chance to tell their (invariably sell-out) audience why this or that idea by someone else (it can't be their own) is well worth paying attention to. *I Wish I'd Thought Of That* has even created in its own acronym – IWITOT – a new word for the international fundraiser's lexicon. The concept of IWITOT has reverberated around the world and become a byword for learning from the creativity and innovation of others. A common reaction from fundraisers leaving an IWITOT event is, 'Who'd have thought fundraising is so creative – I've fallen in love with it, all over again.' And often, 'We could try that!' or, 'Yes, that would work for us, too!' If you can't attend a live IWITOT event – or better still, present the idea you wish you'd thought of at one – hopefully this book will provide you with similar motivation.

IWITOT is no mere celebration of the past. It's about bringing forward great ideas from fundraising's past so they can be the big ideas of our present and the big ideas of our future. It's a kind of big ideas recycling. It's about not neglecting past ideas and leaving them to wither and fade. Instead, it's dedicated to grabbing hold of them, bringing them out into the bright light of understanding and appreciation so that they can be reused again and again and again. Because we know they will work.

CELEBRATING THE SECOND OLDEST PROFESSION

Successful fundraising organisations invest money, time and resources in developing the understanding, skills, knowledge and leadership of the people they employ to ensure fundraising and campaigning success. This book seeks to capture the astonishing breadth and richness of opportunities that campaigning fundraising presents for those seeking a fulfilling career where they can make a difference plus earn a decent living while relishing the challenges, scope, diversity and sheer joy of their chosen occupation.

Fundraising may be the world's second oldest profession, for the sources of the earliest campaign that I'm aware of are none other than the Torah and the Old Testament of the Christian bible. The first recorded mention of fundraising comes from the shared Jewish and Christian tradition, the story of Moses and the children of Israel, which contains an enlightening account of substantial fundraising success recorded 3,500 years ago or more (for sure other religions have their instructive fundraising stories too, see exhibit 8). My career was already well into its second half before I discovered any of this.

When I started as a fundraiser there was no readily available body of fundraising best practice nor was it considered widely as an appropriate occupation for any ambitious youngster. Britain had no association of fundraisers. There were no journals, no conferences, few good books in the UK at least, almost no research or academic study, no internet, no social media, no online libraries, no nothing really. So, in a sense ours is a very new profession too. Now there are all these things and, if anything, there's much too much of them, for questionable advice and misleading information abound. The purpose of this book is to be an antidote to that, to focus on the keys and to identify just what the aspiring world-changer *really* needs to know.

For despite some early career successes (thanks to luck at least as much as to judgement) it was only when I started to unearth the rich history of fundraising that I really began to learn. So, hat-tip to Dr Neil MacGregor of the British Museum, who in his book and radio programme *A History of the World in 100 Objects* showed us a short, structured selection of what matters most from the past and where to find out more about it. His book was the inspiration for what we aim to do here – to gain a revised, richer understanding as our colourful, illustrious past reveals its influence on what's most successful in our present. From this, we'll begin the imaginative, highly productive exercise of creating our future.

Black Lives Matter protester Patrick Hutchinson rescues far right anti-BLM demonstrator Bryn Male at a BLM march in London, June 2020, and carries him to safety. Doing good/ helping others in need is its own justification. It comes naturally to our species. The market for it is infinite.
Photograph: Dylan Martinez/ Reuters.

A SNAPSHOT AT A MOMENT IN TIME

It's to be hoped that fundraisers campaigning for social good are on a trajectory that learns more and gets ever more effective over time. Hopefully we can be as successful as, for example, those fellow innovators of ours who aspired to generate better artificial lighting. Through diligent improvements the earlier lighting pioneers were eventually able to leave far behind the heavy labour and stink of pig fat that once seemed their inevitable lot, until they could jettison tallow candles and move forward to their very own lightbulb moment. I think we're at a similar pivotal point.

According to economist, journalist and broadcaster Tim Harford the cost of generating light has fallen by 500,000 times. Woo-Hoo! Once too precious to use, electric light is now too cheap to notice, but its significance for our species remains profound. Over the centuries the means of generating light in our darkness have become steadily better and cheaper, from the 60 hours of work gathering and chopping wood required to produce light equivalent to just one modern bulb shining for less than a single hour, through to the unpleasant work making tallow candles which, while rendering life a little easier, produced a mere two hours of malodorous, fume-filled fug each evening for a year, at the cost of a whole week of this horrid work. For gloomy ages our society had to depend upon these expensive, labour-intensive technologies and the weak, wobbly light they produced until along came Thomas Edison and his lightbulb. Then everything changed, giving our species easy access to cheap light whenever it's wanted, 24/7. (Here I should also reference the alarming downside of light pollution and its potential to blight lives – another social ill that campaigning fundraisers will no doubt address, in time.) For more lightbulb moments please see exhibit 22.

It's to be hoped that sometime soon, improvements in the processes of campaigning and fundraising for social change will be found that will have a similar quantum of impact. This may seem unlikely now but for sure it's not impossible. In fact, the keys to unlocking such success may already be within our grasp. That, really, is what this book is about.

WE CAN DO BETTER

Our sector could once proudly boast that we were self-regulating – which of course implies that we should own our own responsibility and visibly lead the way rather than waiting for others to do it for us. After UK fundraising's catastrophe – the media's sustained evisceration of bad fundraising practices that started in 2015 – regulation was imposed upon the UK fundraising community from outside, insisted upon by government (again, see exhibits 13 and 22 for the background to this). If we now can get right the fundamental basis for the new era of responsible fundraising, regulation will fall into place and become academic, almost incidental. That will be greatly to the benefit of everyone.

> **'Not only does voluntary service act as a nursery school of democracy, but also as the field in which good neighbourliness may be exercised...fortunately the impulse is wider than the bounds of formal religion, for there never has been greater need than in our own day for the spirit of good neighbourliness among the people at large.'**
>
> *The Nathan Report*, The Committee on the Law and Practice relating to Charitable Trusts, 1952

> **'History is a lively abode, full of surprises.'**
>
> Erik Larsen, *The Splendid and the Vile*, 2020

Though I appreciate that some will wrestle with the concept of the campaigning fundraiser, I don't want to disappear up my own argument in excessively over-analysing the point. My purpose is not to build a scientifically robust case for it, simply to make the point for all fundraisers, particularly for new fundraisers, that they need to see what they do more roundly, not just as the raiser of funds, as their current descriptor suggests. This change will give them pride, commitment and enhanced purpose while reassuring donors and the public about the real role they fulfil.

'The campaigning fundraiser' is not a new breed, though for some it may be a new way of looking at things. In *Relationship Fundraising*, (a book I wrote back in 1992 with help from several visionary fundraisers, particularly Giles Pegram CBE) I urged all fundraisers to think of themselves as relationship fundraisers, with the remit to help their donors to build the best, most mutually advantageous and meaningful relationships with their cause and – as I later came to realise was so, so significant – to deliver consistently the best possible supporter experience to all their donors.

That did involve a new breed of fundraiser. To clarify, I believe fundraisers should see themselves also as campaigning fundraisers, which is not in any way to replace relationship fundraising, but instead adds in the campaigning dimension because it is so central to why the donor is there. They're not there to give us money. They're there to make a difference, to change the world. If we don't include that dimension, fundraising becomes all about the money, and as you'll see from exhibit 22, look where that led us in 2015.

What campaigning fundraising really isn't about

> **Fundraising isn't about money.**
> **It's about work that urgently needs doing.**
> **Don't focus on the money, focus on the people who are sending it.**
> **It's about one person talking to another about something they both care deeply about.**
> **It's about inspiring people to believe they can make a difference, then helping them to make it.**
> **It's about building sustainable, mutually beneficial long-term relationships that deliver lifetime value to both donor and cause.**
>
> From a GIF on Ken Burnett's website www.kenburnett.com

Something else fundraising is not about is easy solutions and soft options. People often dismiss relationship fundraising and the donor-based approach, also referred to as donor-focused fundraising or donor-love, as a warm, fuzzy preference that can disguise fundraising ineffectiveness. The opposite is the case, as even the most cursory review of this book will clearly show.

> **'You should be aware that donor relationship development is not a soft option behind which you can hide a lack of fundraising success. Donor development doesn't amount to a hill of beans unless it leads to more funds raised in the long term. The truth is donor development is all about raising more money. It differs from the hard-sell school of fundraising in that it recognises that because giving is voluntary, raising the maximum funds calls for rare, complex and diverse skills and abilities…donor development is a precision tool that takes us right to the heart of our donors, not a blunt tool with which to bludgeon them.'**
>
> From the introduction to *The Zen of Fundraising* by Ken Burnett, 2006

Fundraising certainly isn't about reinventing the wheel, over and over again. Or at least, it shouldn't be. Fundraising is the natural home for the creative plagiarist. So, it's also about quotable quotes and ideas worth pinching. As a committed magpie I nick good ideas wherever I find them, so this book is full of good ideas of which only a very few are mine. Plagiarism, of course, is the sincerest form of flattery – provided we enhance rather than diminish the original inspirational idea.[2]

So, here are a few more top tips and borrowable phrases that I've benefitted from, that I'd like to squeeze in here so you can borrow them too.

David Ogilvy inspired this saying, which I use all the time.

'The difference between a good fundraiser and a great fundraiser is that the great fundraiser simply knows more. That's all.'

Appropriately to the purpose of this book, he also said.

'If you think education is expensive, try ignorance.'

Alan Clayton gave me the following ten-word slogan. None of these words has more than two letters, yet it's a good mantra for life.

'If it is to be, it is up to me.'

Here's one that I gave him.

'Good enough is, simply, not good enough.'

Such sayings may sound trite or overly simple, but in my experience they're well worth thinking on and acting on too. They can be transformational.

Here are three more:

'Fundraising has to be built on principles and values. The cornerstone of fundraising is consistent integrity.'

'Fundraising has two 'i's. They should stand for innovation and inspiration, not for imitation and irritation.'

'You'll know your donor-focused thinking is making progress when

2 See page 202 for the author's policy regarding copyrights and permissions

you stop saying, "we do this", and start saying, "this is what you make possible".'

Plus, three time-tested old marketing sayings that help us to listen more carefully and to see more clearly:

- **When a customer buys a quarter-inch drill, what he really wants is a quarter-inch hole.**
- **It doesn't matter what you want to sell. The only thing that matters is what they want to buy.**
- **People don't read advertisements. They read what interests them. Sometimes, that includes an advertisement.**

And finally,

The basics matter most. Do your homework. Thoroughly.

I don't know where that last thought comes from, though I expect my teachers at school tried to beat it into my all-but-empty teenage head on an almost daily basis more than half a century ago. I was just too foolish to listen, too impatient to get on to something new. So, I didn't do my homework. Yet despite my personal shortcomings I would respectfully request that from now on, every fundraiser everywhere should be required, if they wish to continue on their career path, to ensure they have a ready familiarity with the basics of their trade and a fair facility with the key developments that form our colourful history. See exhibit 3 in this book. Sushi chefs, judo students and just about every trade or profession you care to name all require their new recruits to attain clearly defined basic standards before they are unleashed upon their publics. Moreover, it's the best way to reveal those who have the natural characteristics, aptitude and skillset that will underpin the genuine love of their calling that makes a great campaigning fundraiser. Yet fundraisers still have no formal requirement to be proficient in the basics. We should change this, now.

That said, on now to my view of how to find the essence of campaigning fundraising from the 52 'exhibits' and the 199 web links I've chosen.

PART 1

Some foundations of campaigning fundraising

All the world's a stage, so Will Shakespeare told us, upon which we mere players must each play our part. As all performers and audience members the world over know only too well, if you fluff your entrance, recovery can be seriously difficult, even impossible. So, before facing those footlights it's sensible to spend time on preparation and rehearsal. And even the most thorough preparation will be all but useless if you don't first understand the essence of what the part you're playing is really all about.

There's no substitute for a good grounding, for 'knowing your onions' as the saying goes. It may not matter much whether or not you know that this popular phrase derives from the noted grammarian and lexicographer Charles Talbot Onions (1873–1965), former editor of the *Oxford English Dictionary*, or from some other source, or indeed that the source is obscure, disputed and uncertain. What's unarguable is that a thorough knowledge of the key issues that matter most to you and your career will surely give you an edge over others who don't know, who perhaps haven't even thought about it or realised how much it matters. For sure, it's hugely important to you that you know enough to make the most of your entrance, so that you can powerfully and effectively deliver and achieve your desired impression; so that you get off to the best possible start.

Junior fundraisers are not routinely inspired or supported enough when first entering this field, yet failure to give new entrants a sufficient grounding leads to massive waste and disappointment. Turnover of fresh talent in the for-change sector – also known as the not-for-profit, charity or voluntary sector – is far too high to be healthy or desirable across almost all developed and emerging fundraising markets. Contributing massively to this is a lack of common entry standards and limited appreciation of what new fundraisers really should know. To reduce this wasteful, damaging turnover, campaigning fundraisers need to ensure that every entrant gets a better grounding in the basics, starting now.

So, in this section you'll find just six of the most important principles of campaigning fundraising, the essentials of which – in my view – any new entrant to this unique, particular business area should seek to secure a firm grasp. These are expanded upon throughout this book and form the foundations upon which future success in their chosen career area will be built.

1 The inspiration business: what campaigning fundraising is for

WHY I CHOSE THIS

Partly at least because the first should be the most important. In his exquisite novella *Le Petit Prince* the French aviator and author Antoine de Saint-Exupéry is clearly exasperated by the inability of grown-ups to see what's truly important. He explains why the little prince prefers the unsullied imaginations of children to the harsh realism of adults. In the illuminating advice he provides below, Saint-Exupéry puts it rather well when he identifies how to go about inspiring people of all ages to achieve extraordinary things. It's a fitting metaphor for the role of the campaigning fundraiser, for this, surely, is the inspiration business.

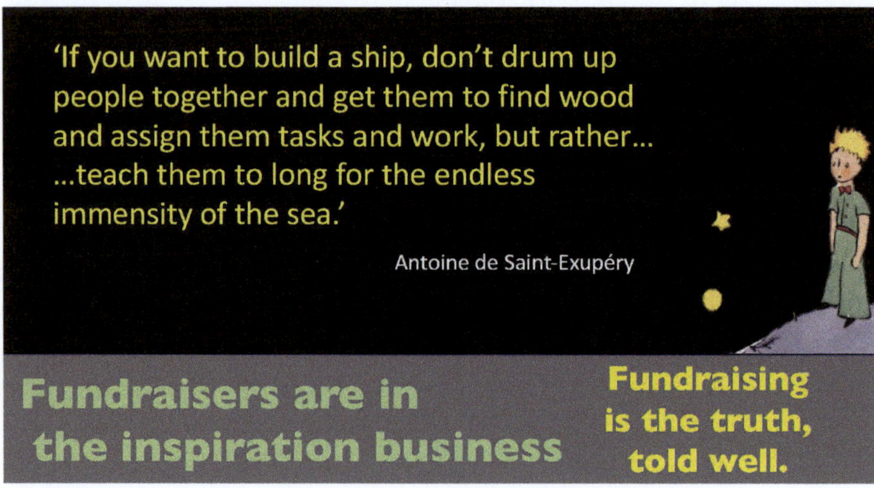

ORIGINS AND OBJECTIVES

I don't know when or where fundraising was first described as the inspiration business, but it's unquestionably the best possible descriptor. Giving is voluntary. It absolutely has to be, or it will simply stop. Fundraisers have no tangible goods or services to sell. No one imagines they need the specific benefits we promote, or at least they can so, so easily convince themselves otherwise. Our task, always, is to inspire them to see that giving is a good thing to do, it's effective, giving a small portion from their finite disposable income is something they really should prioritise, persist in, truly enjoy and benefit from. We encourage and help people to see this. Ours, irrefutably, is the inspiration business.

SIGNIFICANCE AND SPECIAL CHARACTERISTICS

The importance of recognising and celebrating this cannot be over-emphasised. It changes everything, for it redefines the fundraiser's job. Fundraising is always a results-driven business. The best way to get the results you need long term is to keep your donors happy, engaged and inspired. Inspirational fundraising messages work best when they show a clear problem and how the donor can directly be part of the solution. That calls for the powerful motivation that comes from inspiration. Asking for money has little to do with it, neither has pressure, guilt or persuasion.

BACKGROUND STORY

I didn't begin to appreciate this until mid-way through my first fundraising role, when I had the chance to visit Africa to see first-hand ActionAid's work in Kenya and Burundi. I'd already been in my role as head of fundraising at ActionAid for nearly a year. But that first visit and the stories I bumped into while there magnified my effectiveness as a fundraiser at least a hundredfold. I met so many positive people delivering so many tangible success stories and touching so many lives so positively that I realised that, if I could only have my donors there with me, sitting on my shoulders seeing what I was seeing, fundraising success would inevitably be assured. As that was clearly impossible I had to learn to take the magic, the engagement and inspiration, to them, to tell my stories of need and achievement, challenge and solutions with power and passion that would make my readers and listeners' hearts soar and move them inevitably to action. In short, I had to learn to tell the truth, very well.

IMPACT, INFLUENCE AND OPPORTUNITIES

Understanding that our job is to inspire, not to cajole, persuade or plead, is utterly, liberatingly transformational for everyone of any age or level of experience who does this job, wherever they may be. It changes everything we do.

All fundraisers seek repeat giving – it signals that a responder has become a real donor. The key question donors ask is, 'Did my gift get through and did it make a difference?' Answering this requires that we consistently furnish donors with inspirational feedback – what I call the five Fs. Fundraisers should aspire to be famous for frequent, fast, fabulous feedback. In the post-gift

THE 5 Fs:

FAMOUS FOR FREQUENT FAST FABULOUS FEEDBACK

feedback that we should routinely provide (that often we don't do nearly well enough) we have a chance to change our publics' view of fundraising, so that they too see our work as the inspiration business, just as we do. Now, wouldn't that be something? Success at this would multiply our effectiveness and our job satisfaction, no doubt. As Roger Craver says in his foreword, fundraisers often fear they will clear a room at a party just by telling people what they do for a living. Rebuilding the public's understanding and perception of our sector and its key roles would be hugely worthwhile in so many ways.

Inspiration is not just where we start, it has to flow through everything we do, because that's what leads to the impact we and our donors want to see. I've borrowed this handy mnemonic from Michelle Berriman, executive director of the Fundraising Institute of New Zealand, so you can see at a glance where inspiration takes us. As well as having pride in the range, depth and functions of our voluntary sector we should be so, so proud of what we do in fuelling all the benefits that our donors make possible. Viewing and positioning ourselves as the inspiration business will help others to see that too – donors, potential donors and colleagues included.

'Changing the world is the only fit work for a grown man or woman.'

Howard Luck Gossage, quirky, game-changing US adman

LINKS TO MORE ON THE INSPIRATION BUSINESS

https://sofii.org/article/cde-project-6-the-starfish-story

https://sofii.org/article/im-a-fundraiser-because

https://sofii.org/article/the-collection-its-never-too-late-to-do-something-wonderful

HOW THE AGITATOR SEES IT:

http://agitator.thedonorvoice.com/when-founders-leave

2 Building the dream for donors: creating your own Sleeping Beauty's palace

WHY I CHOSE THIS

For donors, the decision to give from their limited disposable income demands a leap of faith based on trust, confidence and optimism. It requires that they believe in and buy into the dream the campaigning fundraiser is revealing, sufficiently to subscribe to it personally with their own limited disposable funds. For years I've illustrated this with a metaphor I found in a story I picked up while listening to the radio, ages ago.

ORIGINS AND OBJECTIVES

The story and its lesson come from the mid-1950s, from the creation of Disneyland, the first large-scale fantasy theme park, established just outside Anaheim, California. Its purpose was to motivate and inspire everyone working on that project, but it's easily adaptable to your projects too.

SIGNIFICANCE AND SPECIAL CHARACTERISTICS

Telling this story while showing the two images above next to the simple quote helps me to explain that, while remaining consistent in its character and content, the dream has to be immediately recognisable from any perspective. The story presents a quick, easily understood and instantly effective way of illustrating the need to keep the organisational dream prominent, clear and consistent yet flexible, fresh and appropriate for all audiences. Not an easy task, sure. But quite achievable for any good communicator.

BACKGROUND STORY

Just before the start of the Disneyland project its creator Walt Disney called a meeting to which he invited all the suppliers, builders, architects, plumbers, electricians and representatives of other assorted trades who collectively would make the Disneyland vision come to life. Eager and excited they assembled before him to hear what their eccentric, visionary boss had to say. Walt then baldly announced to his astonished audience that the very first thing they were going to do was to build Sleeping Beauty's palace, right there, in the centre of the lot.

'Oh no,' cried the architects, plumbers, builders and sundry contractors with one voice, 'we can't do that. First, we have to put in the infrastructure, dig the foundations, lay the electric cabling, put down the sewers, install the...'

Walt Disney was having none of this. He interrupted his agitated advisers and bade them be silent.

'No,' Walt said firmly. 'No. That's not what we're going to do.

'The very first thing we're going to do is to build Sleeping Beauty's palace right here in the centre of the lot, because that, my friends, is the dream. And right from the start, everyone must see the dream. Big, bold, colourful. Right here, now and throughout this great project.

'So,' he explained, 'wherever they might be on this site at whatever time of the night or day, all of the hundreds of people who will work long and hard to make this dream come real, all they each have to do to see the dream, our dream, the reason why we are all here, is to raise their eyes. Without fail they'll see it. The magical, inspirational sight of Sleeping Beauty's palace will keep them constantly focused on and committed to the dream that is Disneyland, right here, at the heart of our theme park.'

And so it was. In years to come the people who worked at Disneyland came to realise that Walt's vision had given them a fabulous metaphor for something all causes, campaigns, movements and even companies must strive to build for their members and customers – to create the dream. It has to be a clear, readily identifiable dream that, even when presented in different views, seen from different angles, in differing light, at different times and with different backgrounds, is still the same, consistent, readily recognisable dream.

IMPACT, INFLUENCE AND OPPORTUNITIES

Every cause should seek to rebuild Sleeping Beauty's palace for their different audiences, with every contact. Or at least to remind everyone of it so clearly, so powerfully that all can see it, even with their eyes closed. To help them achieve this, young fundraisers need to be quickly and directly exposed to their cause, in 'the field'. You have to dream before your dreams can come true. Fundraisers need to show their donors that the best dreams happen when they're awake.

LINKS TO MORE ON BUILDING THE DREAM FOR DONORS

https://sofii.org/case-study/dream-a-dreams-uncrush-a-dream-campaign
https://sofii.org/article/how-i-wrote-it-the-make-a-wish-foundations-prospect-letter
https://sofii.org/article/emotional-fundraising-must-be-in-our-dna

3 The essential foundations of fundraising: why mastering them matters

WHY I CHOSE THIS

For goodness sake, these shouldn't ever have been optional. This is something we really need to change, now. These foundations are called the basics, but they're actually the bedrock. Unless we're prepared to leave the success and direction of our enterprises entirely to chance, every fundraiser everywhere as a matter of course should be required to steep themselves in what is their lifeblood, the basic essentials of their role. Here's where to find at least the bare minimum of what they each need to know.

ORIGINS AND OBJECTIVES

As any chef, home decorator, seminar presenter or a hundred other tradesmen or women worth their salt will know only too well, preparation is key to success. It's often the most important time spent on any task. Getting the thinking right from the start gives you the edge over all others.

From the outset of my fundraising and campaigning adventures I started to write down some of the wise sayings of my mentor, Harold Sumption. Harold was architect of Oxfam's early advertising success and an experienced, brilliantly instinctive relationship fundraiser. He went on to found the annual International Fundraising Congress in Holland, arguably the best conference of its kind in the world, a move that led to the formation of the Resource Alliance. Harold died in 1998. This list of the fundamental foundations of fundraising first appeared three decades ago in *Relationship Fundraising*.

SIGNIFICANCE AND SPECIAL CHARACTERISTICS

A glance at any conference agenda will quickly illustrate the breadth, depth and range of subjects in which today's campaigning and communicating fundraiser has to achieve proficiency. Yet the automatic question 'where do I start?' shouldn't be too difficult to answer. Our unique business area may have become increasingly diverse and complex, yet that very uniqueness demands that certain key considerations have to be understood and absorbed into the DNA of all who work in it if they are to have any hope

#31 Learn the lessons of history
#6 Be a donor
#12 Inspire them to give
#19 Transformational storytelling
#25 Always be honest
#9 Open their hearts
#2 Friend making comes before fundraising
#33 Invest time & money
34
TREEHOUSE of KNOWLEDGE
#30 Say 'thank you'
Discover the fundamental foundations of fundraising at:
sofii.org/article/thetreehouseofknowledge
Commissioned by sofii. Created by A♡G and jessicaraegordon.com
March 2021

of being effective. This list isn't the only such source of course – see the second link below for a couple more of mine – but it was intended to be the one list that should be displayed in every fundraising workplace, showing what matters most to new fundraisers. SOFII has recently produced a poster featuring the entire list, for easy download.

BACKGROUND STORY

Always popular, often quoted, the list featured here has been added to and revised a bit over the years and now as *The Treehouse of Knowledge – the 34 fundamental foundations of fundraising*, it's been one of the most visited areas on SOFII since its inception.

Many fundraisers tell SOFII that they've posted a copy of the 34 fundamental foundations of fundraising prominently on the wall of their fundraising office. Fundraising offices often strike visitors as dull, even dismal places so it's a useful practice to decorate your walls and corridors with helpful, inspirational prompts. These foundations should certainly be there, along with anything else that fundraisers and their managers believe should be kept front of mind or that will inspire and inform their team, and so help them to stand out from other, seemingly similar enterprises. A welcoming workspace is highly conducive to efficiency and effectiveness, so decorating the office walls with inspiration should be a priority. Adding a few exotic plants and impressive pictures helps too, of course. Plus, maybe, some easy chairs, a pool table, a jacuzzi and...

IMPACT, INFLUENCE AND OPPORTUNITIES

Many of fundraising's shortcomings can be attributed to not enough preparation time added to a failure to adequately spread and inculcate a deep, rich understanding of this

The five great assumptions that underpin effective fundraising

- Donors, usually, are generous and caring people.
- They are intelligent, so know when they're being taken advantage of.
- They expect to be treated courteously.
- They are individuals, therefore are varied in their interests, habits and responses.
- They are most likely to respond better when they get from us what they want to receive, rather than what we want them to have.

undoubtedly complex business area. How much more effective would we be if every fundraiser, new and seasoned, could be always aware of and proficient in their understanding of and their facility with the basic tenets of their art and craft? The 34 fundamentals have been refined over time and are rarely challenged. They will, in time, be expanded, even redefined. They will always repay time invested in their appreciation and promotion.

For more on the basics of this trade see also the 11 pillars of fundraising wisdom and the five assumptions that underpin our donor relationships, linked below. In crafting the pillars and assumptions I took inspiration from T E Lawrence, better known as Lawrence of Arabia. The title of his weighty yet seminal work *The Seven Pillars of Wisdom* comes from the Bible, the Book of Proverbs, 9:1, which says 'Wisdom hath builded her house, she hath hewn out her seven pillars.' On reflection I felt fundraising has scope for more than seven pillars, which is debatable, but the principle that we should build our foundations on strong pillars has never left me. What happened to Lawrence's first go at this mighty subject is explained in the link below, and it's worth following just for that.

LINKS TO MORE ON THE ESSENTIAL FOUNDATIONS OF FUNDRAISING

https://sofii.org/article/thetreehouseofknowledge

https://sofii.org/article/the-11-pillars-of-fundraising-wisdom-plus-the-five-assumptions-that-underpin-effective-fundraising

HOW THE AGITATOR SEES IT:

http://agitator.thedonorvoice.com/barriers-to-growth-cliff-notes-edition

4 Reciprocity: if they wish to get, fundraisers first have to give

WHY I CHOSE THIS

Before you get, you have to give. Simple. But so often neglected and misunderstood.

ORIGINS AND OBJECTIVES

It's so easy to imagine fundraising is 'donors give, charities get'. That's the way it's been seen by so many for so long. Yet that's so, so wrong. Giving just doesn't work like that. Looking back, I now realise that I'd learned this at a very young age, but I didn't appreciate its paramount importance until my career was nearing its end. That alone should have taught me something.

SIGNIFICANCE AND SPECIAL CHARACTERISTICS

Again, it's impossible to overstate the importance of this. So please relate this story to all your colleagues. Anyone who then still doesn't get it maybe should look for a different job.

BACKGROUND STORY

Several decades ago, when I was a small boy in short trousers growing up in the North of Scotland, my mother was then area secretary for the charity Dr Barnardo's Homes (a voluntary role). It was Mum's job to dish out their distinctive 'cottage' collecting box to as many households as would take one, then twice each year she'd put an ad in the local paper and invite boxholders to bring their box to our house so we could gather the money they'd collected, for the orphans and the unhappy children. She was big-hearted, my mum. So all the kids from miles around would come to our house clutching their distinctive Barnardo's boxes to have their contents totted up.

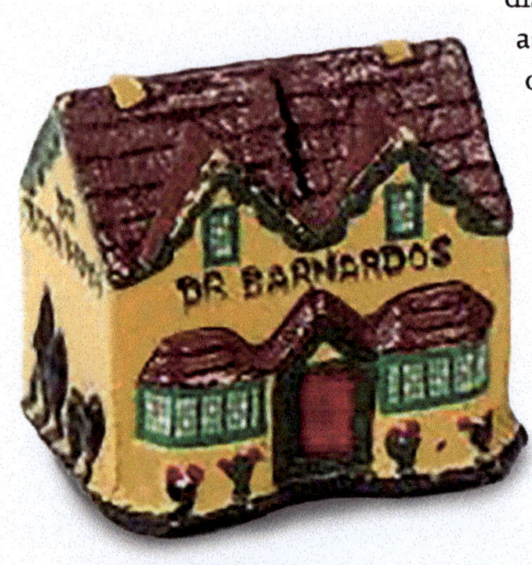

It was my job, aged six or seven, to count the coppers and odd thruppenny bits into shilling piles. Lots of money! I loved it.

But even back then there were so, so many other worthwhile causes all competing for home collectors. So, my mum hit upon a genius idea. She offered each child bringing in a box a piece of her home-made fudge, as a reward.

Now my mum made the world's best fudge. Word spread and soon kids of all ages (and some grown-ups too) were queuing outside our front door, along the path, past the garden gate, round the corner and down our street, all clutching their colourful boxes ready for emptying. I had to work twice as hard at the emptying out and totting up. So, I thought, a piece of fudge for you for bringing in the box, a piece of fudge for me, for counting it.

It was only fair.

My mother grew to be one of the top fundraisers in the North of Scotland for Dr Barnardo's Homes. I grew to be a rather large child, from too much fudge. But it was here that I learned the value of reciprocity. The more you give, the more you get too. And it's surprising just how many opportunities there are for fundraisers and storytellers to give as well as get. It doesn't need to be much, or even anything tangible. A warm sense of satisfaction will suffice. If nothing else, the fundraiser should always leave the donor with a moving emotional story of what their support will achieve. For many people, that's memorable and priceless.

IMPACT, INFLUENCE AND OPPORTUNITIES

If charities would only commit to giving as much as they get, donors would stay longer and give more too. Generosity is not just reciprocal, it's also infectious. We should make more of this. So, remember Dr Barnardo's and perfect and promote your commitment to the 5Fs, see exhibit 1.

LINKS TO MORE ON RECIPROCITY

https://sofii.org/case-study/dr-barnardos-home-the-home-collecting-box

https://www.youtube.com/
watch?v=wYCB10WYZvM&amp=&feature=youtu.be

HOW THE AGITATOR SEES IT:

http://agitator.thedonorvoice.com/the-power-of-reciprocity

5 Learning to look: why donors need to give, as much as they give to need

WHY I CHOSE THIS

This exhibit shows that it pays big time to learn to look at opportunities in the right way. It's a skill so worth perfecting.

SIGNIFICANCE AND SPECIAL CHARACTERISTICS

It's perhaps one of the world's oldest and cheesiest truisms – glass half full, or half empty? – but the Bata Shoes story remains a sure guide for aspiring fundraisers. It sets out a philosophy on life that will never leave you. Its origins may even be apocryphal but the evidence that it works is all over East Africa and its lessons are as relevant today as ever.

ORIGINS AND BACKGROUND

When first I visited Africa in 1978, touring the wild north of Kenya, I kept seeing in the tiny villages and markets along the way signs for Bata, the shoe company. When it came to indications of commercial product dominance in these fly-blown, out of the way spots, Bata was in evidence far more than any other maker of anything. I wondered why at the time and later was told this tale in explanation.

At the turn of the 19th century, just as colonial Africa was opening up as a market, all the manufacturers of shoes in Victorian England sent their representatives to Africa to see if there might be an opportunity there for them to sell their wares.

Photo credit: the Captain Tom Foundation and Emma Sohl, Capture the Light Photography

Captain Tom Moore sets out to raise £1,000 by walking round his garden. He eventually raised more than £32 million.

All duly came back in time with the same answer. 'Nobody in Africa wears shoes. So, there is no market for our products there.'

All, that is, save for the Bata rep. He came back saying, 'Nobody in Africa wears shoes. So, there's a huge market for our products in Africa!' All had seen the same thing. He just saw it differently.

That's how Bata shoes came to be known as the shoes of Africa. It's why to this day you'll find signs promoting Bata all over Africa, even in the remotest of spots.

IMPACT, INFLUENCE AND OPPORTUNITIES

The Bata Shoes anecdote is therefore a 'glass half full' story, perfect for the positive thinker. Which has to be all fundraisers. Surely someone was thinking along these lines in 2020 when they discovered that world war veteran 99-year-old Captain Tom Moore was planning to raise £1,000 for the UK's National Health Service by walking round his garden to mark his upcoming birthday. Follow the link below for the full story, though surely everyone's heard it by now? For Captain (now Colonel Sir) Tom went on to raise over £32 million from more than 1.5 million individual donors who flocked online to support him.[1] Proof that in a crisis people don't just give to need, they also need to give. Bata can't take direct credit, but the style of thinking is the same. Do cultivate and encourage it. Positive things happen to positive thinkers. It triumphs every time.

LINKS TO MORE ON LEARNING TO LOOK

https://sofii.org/article/the-bata-shoes-story

https://sofii.org/article/fundraising-successes-at-a-time-of-catastrophe

1 Sadly Sir Tom died in 2021 from Covid-19, the coronavirus, and the whole British nation mourned him as a fundraising hero. See more on the importance of the hero figure in fundraising, in exhibit 28.

6 Asking properly: crucially important, as our mum taught us, long ago

WHY I CHOSE THIS

Why do people sometimes struggle with the simplest of concepts? Most probably, it's because in our busy organisations, obsessed by the day-to-day and driven by targets, objectives and organisational expectations, we don't stop often enough or long enough to think about the fundamental principles that should underpin our daily actions. To the dismay and distress of donors and fundraisers alike, in 2015 (see exhibits 13 and 22) the UK fundraising community suffered a near-catastrophic scandal that all but undermined public confidence in charities and their fundraising methods – all because many well-known charity brands had lost sight of some of the most basic tenets of their very existence, including the absolute imperative of asking properly. So, fundraisers need to be reminded of them, constantly.

ORIGINS AND OBJECTIVES

Many of the most basic fundamentals of fundraising and campaigning are, literally, the blindingly obvious. This most of us learned at our mother's knee. But a simple realisation of the central importance of asking properly could have saved British charities £millions – and much distress and heartache – just a few short years ago.

SIGNIFICANCE AND SPECIAL CHARACTERISTICS

George Smith was my business partner for 20 years. When he wrote his definitive guide to creativity in fundraising he gave it the title *Asking Properly* – with very good reason. Here's how he defined that simple act:

'My mother always told me to ask properly for things. I was told off if I was impolite or over-aggressive. I was reprimanded for asking in sloppy language or incomplete sentences. I was scorned for asking for the impossible. I was honoured when, on occasion, I did manage to ask properly.'

George Smith, *Asking Properly*, 1996

Sounds simple enough but of course in practice it seems it's not so easy. Or at least, it's been a nigh insurmountable challenge for fundraisers in many countries around the world. That's right. The simple act of asking properly is something professional fundraisers seem to struggle with, much more than they should.

BACKGROUND STORY

The media onslaught of 2015 that so expensively devastated the UK's fundraising community (with hopefully positive eventual outcomes, see exhibits 13 and 22) showed unarguably that asking properly was something that wasn't routinely happening in far too many fundraising initiatives. We need no more evidence than this, to now commit to getting this right. So, we need to be vigilant. I'm not sure our supporters will forgive us if we allow similar negativity to arise again.

IMPACT, INFLUENCE AND OPPORTUNITIES

A classic example of asking properly can be seen from the Greenpeace Thorp mailing pack from the 1990s, when some ambitious wag in their advertising agency suggested adding to a seemingly routine appeal – in addition to a box for donations of just £0.50p – a cheeky tick box that sought over 2,500 times more than their previous highest prompt. And lo, someone actually ticked that box! Follow the link for this uplifting story. Proof, were it needed, that fifty pence or £250,000, getting the simple act

2. GIVE WHAT YOU CAN AFFORD
The legal bill that now looms so large can be made up from thousands of small amounts. Every gift however large will bring us nearer our target.
And, as British Nuclear Fuels and the Government now know, Greenpeace has many thousands of friends.

Yes, here's my donation

☐ £100 ☐ £50 ☐ £25 ☐ £10 ☐ £0.50 ☐ £250,000!

☐ Other__________

☐ I enclose a cheque/PO payable to Greenpeace Ltd. Please note that Greenpeace is unable to accept charity vouchers or payroll giving.

Dear Dad,

It was so good to hear from Mum and you over the phone. I've made a lot of new friends here at college and I'm not short of things to do. But I do miss home– especially Mum's cooking.

Can I come straight to the point? I need a new computer. The old Amstrad has had its day. It's slow, it's not printing properly and I'm wasting hours shouting at the damned thing. More seriously it's getting in the way of my course work – I've got a 10,000-word thesis on Jack Kerouac to turn in by the end of term and at this rate I'm not going to make it. Worse, anything I produce on it looks crap compared with the professional-looking work that other students are producing. I know you've already spent a small fortune on getting me here – all I can say is that another couple of hundred quid will make a heck of a difference for the next three years.

I've seen a second-hand PC advertised in the college magazine. It's not quite state of the art but it does have Windows 3.0 and a decent printer and it's all I need to see me through to my finals. The bloke wants £300 and I think I can knock him down to £250 if I move fast. I think I can contribute £50 from what I've got in the bank.

So, I'm asking if you can spare another £200. I know it's a lot to ask and I think you know that I wouldn't ask unless it was genuinely important and urgent. If you can't afford it then I'll shut up and soldier on with the Amstrad. But if you can, then it really is going to improve everything I do here. What do you say?

I really need to call this bloke before the weekend (I'm sweating now that no one has made him an offer in the meantime). So, if you could call me or, better still, just put a cheque for £200 in first class post, then you'll make my week.

Sorry to be such a pest. All I can offer if you say yes is a beautifully presented, well-worded thesis on Kerouac that I'll happily show you at Christmas and which will make your paternal heart swell with pride.

I can't tell you how much I'm looking forward to Christmas. College is great but there's nothing like family. So, give my love to Mum and Jenny.

Adam

Dear Dad,

Your kind gift of £700 has been safely received and is already at work in buying course textbooks and enabling me to enjoy a full part in the social life of the college. I cannot tell you how grateful I am for your continued support.

I just cannot continue with this clapped-out Amstrad.

A decent PC is vital for today's student. When lessons are over, we typically go back to our rooms and write up our notes. Failure to do so can lead to poor marks, slippage in course work and – all too often – the derision of our fellows. 25 per cent of students fail to complete a degree here. The cause is often an inadequate computer.

I am one such student.

I labour nightly on an Amstrad which is a positive impediment to my academic success.

I ask you to imagine this computer.

It is slow.

Its printer is trouble-prone.

It will not interface with any other known machine.

In short, I risk severe under-achieving. I have to tell you that I just cannot continue with this Amstrad.

Just £200 will make the difference.

Yes, a second-hand PC of the required quality can be procured for just £200. Can you find it in your heart to make such a gift? You have proved yourself such a dutiful parent that I am sure you will want to make this extra investment in the academic future of your first-born son. But please give NOW – every day counts when it comes to vital word-processing. I can only buy this computer with **YOUR** help.

Yours sincerely,

Adam

PS. Why not phone through your response? The need is truly URGENT.
PPS. I cannot tell you how much this gift would mean to me!!!

of asking right will change all our expectations and will vastly augment whatever we think we have a right to expect.

Now campaigning fundraisers face a great opportunity to redefine what asking properly really means. George Smith made a heroic start in this while writing about creative messaging. The Supporter Experience Project of the UK's Chartered Institute of Fundraising is also taking this on, building upon the findings of the Commission on the Donor Experience, who completed their 28 detailed projects in 2017 and produced *The 6Ps* document (see exhibit 22). But all fundraisers should be aware that this is still very much a work in progress, and their help is needed to truly deliver exemplary supporter experiences to all the world's donors. Now, there's an opportunity indeed...

LINKS TO MORE ON ASKING PROPERLY

https://sofii.org/case-study/greenpeaces-optimistic-tick-box-suggestion-the-stop-thorp-campaign-court-case-mailing

https://sofii.org/article/ask-without-fear-a-simple-guide-to-connecting-donors-with-what-matters-to-them-most

https://sofii.org/article/a-letter-that-parades-fine-thoughts-with-fine-language

https://sofii.org/article/the-olive-cooke-story

HOW THE AGITATOR SEES IT:

http://agitator.thedonorvoice.com/what-ask-string-works-best

Opposite: Sincerity and substance vs technique and formulae. Which seems most real? Which will work best? Courtesy of George Smith and *Asking Properly*, an instructive parody in two parts – the second version opposite illustrates how fundraisers often ask for money in a strange, over-inflated and quite unnatural style.

PART 2

Lessons from the history of campaigning fundraising

If you don't know where you've been, chances are you won't know where you are or where you're going. Campaigning fundraising has a rich history and tradition of innovation and enterprise that underpins the standards and best practices of today's successful fundraising organisations. Should new recruits to this unique business be lucky enough to discover the depth and breadth of this, they'll be surprised and delighted. Seasoned older hands too. What's tragic is that so many fundraisers are only likely to discover their history by chance, as it's poorly understood and under-appreciated within the sector. As a result, few of the potential lessons from our colourful, instructive past are ever realised.

Our sector should seek to change this, so that we might avoid the all-too-frequent equivalent of reinventing the wheel and also position ourselves to appreciate and celebrate the benefits of creative plagiarism. Why trouble to think of your own big idea if you can borrow (and hopefully embellish) someone else's? We'll save time and rise higher if we commit to doing this, properly.

In this section you'll find brief introductions to much of campaigning fundraising's fertile, varied hinterland of history, with multiple links to take you deeper into the many benefits of learning from our instructive past. In choosing what to include we've been obliged to leave out many gems, but hopefully that'll merely enhance your curiosity and pleasure from further searches, as you follow the links provided.

7 Our early history: rich rewards from spending time with the ancients

WHY I CHOSE THIS

The Greeks invented the word philanthropy as part of the human quest for excellence. The Romans, according to the poet Benjamin Zephaniah, invented welfare, though for long generations before then families and villages across Africa already had sophisticated systems and culture for supporting society's weakest. The Romans also placed a high premium on justice, clemency and caring for the disadvantaged and in their way were dab hands at fundraising and campaigning. As a young fundraiser I didn't know this and I suspect, neither do most fundraisers today. Yet, as can be seen, there's such a lot to learn from the Greeks, the Romans and other early civic enthusiasts. Pioneers in China, Africa, the Middle East and elsewhere too, no doubt.

ORIGINS, OBJECTIVES, SIGNIFICANCE AND SPECIAL CHARACTERISTICS

According to the ancient Greek legend *Prometheus Bound* we are told how the primitive creatures that were created to be human at first had no knowledge, skills, or culture of any kind, so lived in caves, in the dark, in constant fear for their lives. If this description reminds you of a fundraising office you know, I share your pain. But please read on. Zeus, the tyrannical king of the gods, decided to destroy them, so Prometheus, a Titan whose name meant forethought, out of his *philanthropos tropos* or 'humanity-loving character', gave them two empowering, life-enhancing gifts: fire, which symbolises all knowledge, skills, technology, arts and science, and 'blind hope' or 'optimism'. The two went together – with fire, humans could be optimistic; with optimism, they could use fire constructively to improve the human condition. I like that.

BACKGROUND STORY

Philanthropy, if rightly done, forms the glue that holds the Roman people together. So argued Seneca, tutor to the emperor Nero, in his book

On Benefits, composed c.60 BCE (before the common era). From many examples of doing it right from this era on SOFII I've chosen just five, see exhibit 8. Please do find your own favourites by following the links.

Giving has always had social cachet. *The Free Science Encyclopaedia* cites a Jewish example which praises a system where donors could give anonymously and also recipients could receive those donations anonymously, therefore eliminating the possibility of shame for those in need. 'Voluntary donors who act anonymously and who succeed in organizing others in durable networks of mutual aid get highest praise in this literature.' The reference there is to ancient Jewish literature. Jewish culture also gave us the notion that individual donors should, 'give till it hurts'. What a fabulous gift!

Examples of giving, sacrifice and the philanthropy of those who can afford it, from the widow's mite in the Christian bible's New Testament to the mega-rich donors who paid for King Solomon's temple, all have encouraged public generosity, inspired admiration and led to social change ever since our species first started to record the things that matter most. Yet somehow this fertile history has become undervalued and overlooked in too many fundraising offices.

IMPACT, INFLUENCE AND OPPORTUNITIES

The generosity of others can of course lead to disdain and envy, while wealth, of itself, is not despicable, what matters is how people choose to use it. If it's used well, that should be encouraged, not sneered at, particularly when it's used to make things better for others. These are just a few reasons why substantial fundraising campaigns have to be carefully and professionally managed. So, competent professionals are welcome. Fundraising may indeed be the second oldest profession – see the web links in this section and the wealth of great content they're linked to. However, there's also of course ample room for the committed, enthusiastic, gifted amateur.

LINKS TO MORE ON OUR EARLY HISTORY

https://sofii.org/article/philanthropy-in-ancient-times-some-early-examples-from-the-mediterranean

https://sofii.org/foundations-of-fundraising/the-sofii-history-project

8 Five fine firsts: finding valuable lessons in our deep past

WHY I CHOSE THESE

Our history, of course, is inevitably incomplete. We'll perhaps never know who invented the first fundraising shopping list or tested the first addition of a response coupon at the foot of an ad. Though, who knows, perhaps we might?[1] Details of early initiatives emerge frequently. Hopefully the surprising riches and diverse lessons from those recorded here might stimulate the discovery of further finds.

ORIGINS AND OBJECTIVES

We know about the first recorded successful fundraising campaign, though it happened around 3,500 years ago. We can tell of the first major donor dinner, the first matching funds campaign and, perhaps, the earliest recorded example of a fundraising director seeking to rally his troops. We can also share details of a startlingly effective direct mail appeal letter from 800 years ago; though perhaps it's unlikely to be the first letter of its kind, it was until recently the earliest we knew of (*The Agitator* claims to have unearthed an even earlier one, see below). I found out about it just a few years ago from my friend Mal Warwick in Berkeley, California. Mal is himself a legend of fundraising direct mail and author of some of the best books on the subject (see exhibit 17). Eihei Dogen's letter, written in 1235 by a Japanese monk seeking after a long absence to build a monastery in his homeland, is a brilliant near 800-year-old guide to how to do fundraising by direct mail.

SIGNIFICANCE AND SPECIAL CHARACTERISTICS

Despite these treasures, the most surprising thing about our history's many lessons is that so few fundraisers are even vaguely aware of them. Hopefully publicising these five noteworthy firsts might help change that.

BACKGROUND STORIES

* The world's oldest fundraising case history describes how the prophet Moses raised funds for the tabernacle, a mobile church, more than 1,500

1 If you know do please tell. There's a special place on SOFII's home page for new additions.

years BCE. Moses was an accomplished fundraiser who both understood his audience and appreciated the nuances of his fundraising proposition and how it would be received. This appeal so far exceeded target that Moses had to tell many of the enthusiastic volunteers to stop and they even refunded donations to some donors (as it happens, a money-back guarantee can lead to great fundraising, see link below). The case history on SOFII includes a detailed list of the key learning points from this first, very successful campaign.

- For the first recorded (as far as we know) major donor dinner more than 3,000 years ago King David, king of the 12 Jewish tribes, invited the great and the good of the day for an evening at his palace. Over dinner the King launched a challenge appeal to raise the means to build a temple to his son Solomon and ended his pitch with the announcement of his own lead gift. The full target was raised that night – the equivalent in today's money of US$400 million. Not bad for a fundraising first effort.
- St Paul's letter to the Corinthians records the launch of what could be the first ever appeal for regular, committed donors. Paul asked his supporters in the city of Corinth to set aside a small portion of their income regularly, to sustain victims of a famine and then later to support good works generally. The entry on SOFII lists ten clear lessons fundraisers can learn from St Paul's early letters. Who knew?
- In the first ever matched giving appeal Pliny the Younger and his friend Tacitus unlocked local pride and generosity to open a school in Como, Italy, in c.100 BCE. In his writings Pliny the Younger left a detailed record of his life, wealth and generosity, including his letter to Tacitus that launched the world's first known matching funds appeal. This was only a tiny part of his and his contacts' philanthropy.
- For such an early example Eihei Dogen's remarkable letter reveals some impressively good practice. It's not unusual for a direct mail fundraiser to specify his or her target audience in detail and set out precisely why he's writing to them and what he wants them to do. Nor, as he presents his case for support, is it surprising to see the writer appeal to his reader's sense of duty and fairness, to make his case with urgency and reassure donors how their funds will be used. It's good practice to honour donors, to reference naming rights and to appropriately recognise

From the San Francisco Zen Center, a translation of an appeal sent to Buddhist monks throughout Japan in 1235 by Eihei Dogen, monk of the Kannondori Monastery. (The letter was submitted by San Francisco Bay Area fundraising consultant Lisa Hoffman and was translated by Michael Weger and Kazuaki Tanaka.) The letter begins

We respectfully make this announcement to all buddhas in the ten directions, sages and monks in the heavenly and human worlds, the eight types of beings in the dragon realm, generous men and women. We wish to construct a training hall with small donations from people's pure heart.

Now, how's that for targetting the audience?

For some years ever since I returned to Japan from China, I have vowed to establish a monastery. But there has not been a place suitable to support monks' formal practice using bowls and robes. Now we have acquired an excellent place ... Although it is still covered with weeds and not yet functioning, we plan to build a training monastery there ... We urgently need a Monk's Hall right now. We plan to build one seven ken square (70feet square), with no interior walls. We will set up long platforms to reside on, where we will practice day and night without fail...

It's difficult to find a better example in contemporary fundraising letters of a specific justification for the need for money. And did you notice the urgent note in the copy?

Then this note about donor recognition

We will acknowledge gifts by installing the donors' names in the center of the sacred image. The myriad syllables of the seed wisdom will honour the donors and everyone.

The monk closes

Those who will attain the way in this hall will be guiding masters of the assembly, Truly they will be knowledgeable and reach not only the human realm but transform beings in the heavenly realm and in the dragons' palace. Those in the realms of magic and darkness will also listen. Thus this dharma wheel transmitted from Shyakyamuni Buddha can reach everywhere.

Who could possibly resist such a compelling appeal?

each donor's contribution. A good fundraising letter usually ends with a summary of the compelling yet intangible benefits that will come the donor's way, following a generous gift. What is unusual is to find all this in a fundraising appeal letter from 1235.

IMPACT, INFLUENCE AND OPPORTUNITIES

As with all the other firsts or near-firsts, Eihei Dogen's letter is important because, had you known about it in 1235 or indeed in any of the nearly 800 years during which such things became commonplace components of the fundraiser's craft, your appeals, every one of them, would have fared much better than those of your comrades and competitors. That's why these things matter, why familiarity with history is so helpful. It saves so many wheels being reinvented. Following the links below will lead you to more, equally instructive examples from deep history.

The many opportunities that would flow from studying these iconic campaigns are obvious, as Eihei Dogen's unexpected letter again exemplifies. I'd so love to know, what are the eight types of beings in the dragon realm? And how did they use bowls and robes? Perhaps if someone at the time had documented this initiative, we'd know about these things too and our fundraising down the ages would have benefitted appropriately. Not to mention the myriad syllables of seed wisdom – oh how I'd love to fill my writings with those! Truly, history can teach us much. What's here is just the tiniest taste – there's *lots* more...

LINKS TO MORE ON THE FIVE FINE FIRSTS

https://sofii.org/case-study/moses-raises-funds-for-the-tabernacle-c-1-500-bc

https://sofii.org/case-study/the-first-ever-major-donor-dinner-c-970-bc

https://sofii.org/case-study/paul-the-apostle-motivates-his-churchs-donors-c.-56-ad

https://sofii.org/case-study/pliny-the-younger-and-the-first-appeal-for-matching-funds-c-100-ad

https://sofii.org/case-study/eihei-dogen-fundraising-letter-from-1235

https://sofii.org/case-study/habitat-for-humanity-money-back-guarantee

9 The Middle Ages: shaping our understanding of philanthropy

WHY I CHOSE THIS

As Rhodri Davies, head of policy at Charities Aid Foundation, has put it, 'Philanthropy has a long history in the UK. From the mid 1500s, the modern notion of philanthropy, based on secular concerns about poverty and the social issues of the day, emerged to replace the medieval concept of almsgiving, which was all about securing your immortal soul by carrying out your religious duty to give via the church. Since then, philanthropy has played a vital role in shaping the society we live in.'

ORIGINS AND OBJECTIVES

He's right, though securing your immortal soul is still seen as important by many and remains a significant driver of donations. Down the ages, voluntary giving has been essential to how our society has functioned, not just in the West but around the world. Many of the most magnificent cathedrals that sprang up across Europe in the Middle Ages were funded by donations from individuals, often in return for the promise of salvation or under the threat of being boiled in oil. In the social-media equivalent of those times, stories of these monumental achievements must have spread like wildfire, filling the populace with wonder and nurturing a culture of giving for the charitable funding of great works.

SIGNIFICANCE AND SPECIAL CHARACTERISTICS

Stonemasons started building the cathedral of Notre Dame in Paris in 1160 and the church was largely complete less than 200 years later, with the famous flying buttresses added in the 13th century. It's noteworthy that those who designed the church didn't expect to live to see its completion. For them, belief in what they were trying to achieve was enough. The story goes that the first ever time and motion study was carried out among the stonemasons building Notre Dame. The survey organisers, apparently, found three distinct attitudes among the workers:

* The first group thought,
  'I am carving stone blocks into shape, to complete this large building.'
* The second group's view was,
  'I am building what will be a truly magnificent church.'
* The third group believed,

'I am dedicating my working life to the glory of God.'

All were of course doing exactly the same thing as each other, day in, day out. But which group do you imagine worked hardest to complete their task? And which most often called in sick on a Monday morning, complaining of a bad back?

BACKGROUND STORY

Some 50 years or so before the Zen master Eihei Dogen was raising funds to build his monastery in Japan the Jewish scholar Moses Maimonides was developing and refining his definition of *tzedakah*, charity based on fairness and justice, which included the eight levels of giving and the earliest

known reference to a concept that later generations of fundraisers would call *the 90-degree shift* – ie, seeing through your donor's eyes.

Around this time, giving by charitable bequest or legacy was coming to be increasingly popular. In time giving by a legacy (see exhibit 20) would grow to be one of the largest sources of income from individual donors. The will or testament is a universal tool recognised in most societies as a means by which we can take care of affairs, look after our family and friends and fund direct actions by charities after we die. Cultures and countries may enact their own interpretations in law and process but, essentially, we can all use our last will as a vehicle to manage our departure and last wishes. The act of giving through a will is ancient and equally universal. In his book *Foundations for Fundraising* the late great Redmond Mullin describes an appeal for Troyes Cathedral that between 1389 and 1423 – around the time of the battle of Agincourt – received approximately four per cent of its income from legacies. Legacies have long been a trusted way to give.

IMPACT, INFLUENCE AND OPPORTUNITIES

Regular giving (tithing) and legacy giving are time-honoured staples of the fundraiser's toolbox, regularly illuminating for donors the various, most effective ways they can make a difference in this world (see exhibits 19 and 20). Both remain the campaigning fundraiser's best offerings to this day. Yet, perhaps as a consequence of our sector's general ignorance of its history combined with the widespread unwillingness in our organisations to ensure that all recruits must at least possess demonstrable familiarity with the basics of their trade, these tools and their application are still only thinly understood. Which represents a fantastic opportunity for any organisation that wants to do fundraising and campaigning properly and well.

LINKS TO MORE ON FUNDRAISING IN THE MIDDLE AGES

https://sofii.org/article/moses-maimonides-the-90-degree-shift-800-years-ago

https://sofii.org/article/a-timeline-of-modern-british-philanthropy

HOW THE AGITATOR SEES IT:

http://agitator.thedonorvoice.com/the-oldest-profession-in-fundraising

10 The Victorians: sowing the seeds of today's giving culture

WHY I CHOSE THIS

History for fundraisers just gets ever more useful. The great philanthropists of the Victorian age – Olivia Hill, Jeremy Bentham, Lord Shaftesbury, John Stuart Mill, Joseph Rowntree, Florence Nightingale, William Booth, Louisa Twining, Andrew Carnegie and others – are one reason why fundraising history from this era is so rewarding for eager campaigning fundraisers. The social wrongs that so exercised these visionary donors provided an impetus to extraordinary creativity and enterprise. Improved communication among an emerging middle class also helped, plus the religious imperative then prevailing, to rail against poverty, hardship and unfairness. The injustices and inequalities of this period were visible on almost every street corner and for all the increases in voluntary activity their grip on the poor and disadvantaged seemed to spread rather than lessen. Yet for sheer passion and inventiveness the legacy left by Victorian campaigners and fundraisers really repays some study.

BACKGROUND, SIGNIFICANCE AND SPECIAL CHARACTERISTICS

The Victorian era was marked by ingenuity and sweeping progress, a period of social and technological change that affected all aspects of society. According to a study by Warwick and Glasgow universities and the Alan Turing Institute and published in the journal *Nature Human Behaviour*, the year when the British people were happiest was 1880. That may be arguable, but the Victorian era was certainly an epoch rich in charitable enterprise, creative writing, emotional storytelling, innovation and invention with the launch of large-scale movements that galvanised the emerging monied middle classes. Private individuals became increasingly aware of urgent social needs crying out for charitable funds, those feeling guilty from ill-gotten gains could assuage their consciences and those with

scruples were ready to believe that through these evolving new bodies they could make a tangible difference. So, the great causes of the time grew and multiplied.

Throughout the Victorian era, Britain was arguably the world superpower and leader of the explosion in industry and technology that, at least for some, was ushering in a new age of prosperity and advancement. Of course, Victorian Britain had its all-but-overwhelming dark side, with rampant poverty, inequality and widespread deprivation, exploitation and misery. As some prospered while others suffered class divisions became ever more pronounced, which made it a particularly productive time for would-be founders of great causes. The 'magic moments' featured in the articles linked below are not exclusively from the Victorian era, but many are. Lots of the most successful fundraising organisations of the 21st century have their origins in the 19th century.

IMPACT, INFLUENCE AND OPPORTUNITIES

The rallying cry for all emerging causes at this time could well have been, 'absolutely everyone can be a donor – you just need some spare cash and the compassion felt by any civilised individual'. Campaigners of the time latched on to this growing mood of civic responsibility to fundraise and thus shaped a boom in charitable giving that continues to this day. The modern concept of a charity donor was now firmly in place.

LINKS TO MORE ON VICTORIAN FUNDRAISING

https://sofii.org/case-study/dr-barnardos-homes-how-the-death-of-carrots-led-to-a-powerful-slogan-from-1866

https://sofii.org/case-study/the-collection-tin

https://sofii.org/case-study/the-national-trust-recruiting-members-by-the-millions

https://sofii.org/article/magic-moments-how-small-beginnings-inspire-great-causes

11 The 20th century: a legacy of treasures from our recent past

WHY I CHOSE THIS

Queen Victoria died in 1901 but the boom in philanthropy and voluntary action that had so blossomed in her era continued to flourish right through the tumultuous century that followed. As with the previous exhibit, it seemed invidious to choose a single story that defines the campaigning fundraising lessons of an entire century, so I've chosen to illustrate the richness of this era by highlighting just three different campaigns from different times and cultures, because they were either socially transformational or massively successful, or both.

ORIGINS AND OBJECTIVES

These three case histories are indicative of a vast resource which the keen campaigning fundraiser will enjoy exploring. In the process, he or she will uncover useful inspiration and instruction, perhaps along with some recyclable ideas that might prove catalytic in fostering further social change.

SIGNIFICANCE AND SPECIAL CHARACTERISTICS

The term treasures is no hyperbole. The range and diversity are quite astounding. From a cornucopia of inspirational achievements from the last century and confined as always by finite space, these three distinctive campaigns each illustrate commitment, tenacity, courage, and ingenuity, with more besides. I recommend you research among the many linked below, to find your own favourites.

BACKGROUND STORIES

Fundraising's potential for enabling massive social change emerged substantially and securely in the 20th century, aided by a rapidly evolving media landscape. The 20th century's truly world-changing campaigns illustrate the potential for fundraising campaigners, volunteers and professionals alike, to use their skills to really shape society.

✶ **VOTES FOR WOMEN:** Fundraising for the Suffragettes records a social change of such significance that it should be understood by all men and women everywhere. 'Purple stands for the royal colour that flows in the veins

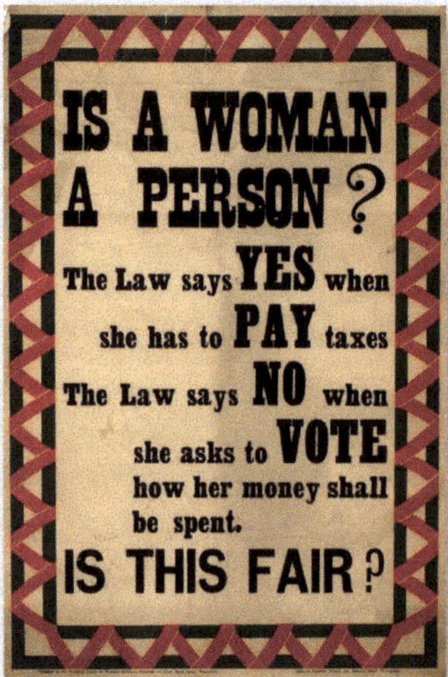

of every suffragette, the instinct of freedom and dignity…white stands for purity in private and public life…green is the colour of hope and the emblem of spring.' So is described the thinking underpinning the choice of colours for the brand identity beneath which a movement united to change forever the political landscape of Britain. And influence the rest of the world.

✶ **BRITAIN'S BIGGEST EVER APPEAL:** My, how those pennies mounted up! In 1946, just after the end of the Second World War, a huge, highly detailed campaign from the British Red Cross raised more than £500 million, which in today's money would be equivalent to around £7.7 billion, making it arguably the most successful fundraising appeal of all time. Significantly the appeal targeted different sectors of society, devising specific approaches and techniques to suit each individual target group. In the process the appeal pioneered many initiatives that are now fundraising staples, such as charity shops, payroll giving, penny-a-week appeals and house-to-house collections. A single aspect of this mega-appeal – the Aid to Russia Fund – provided clothing, blankets, medical supplies and other items to the Soviet Red Cross. It also paid for machinery for two factories in Russia to produce artificial limbs.

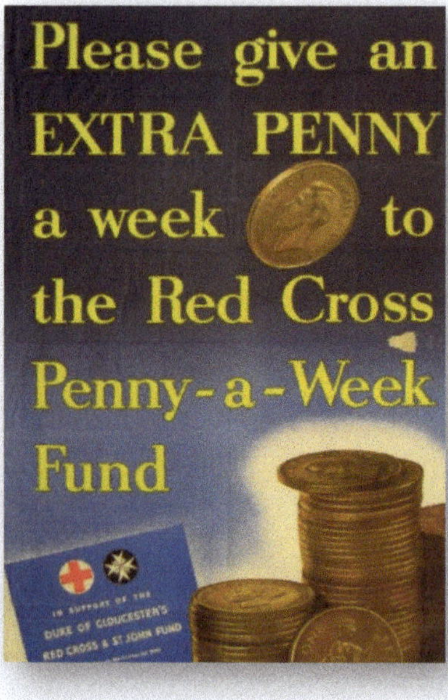

✶ **THE APPEAL LETTER THAT GOT 100 PER CENT RESPONSE:** Just 24 individuals received this singularly well-crafted letter in the 1920s and even though they were required with their response to include a cheque for, at the time, a significant sum, all promptly responded positively. The buzz he got from this triumph launched one of the finest letter-writing careers of all time, as American ad man and soon-to-be master fundraising copywriter Bruce Barton had got the bug!

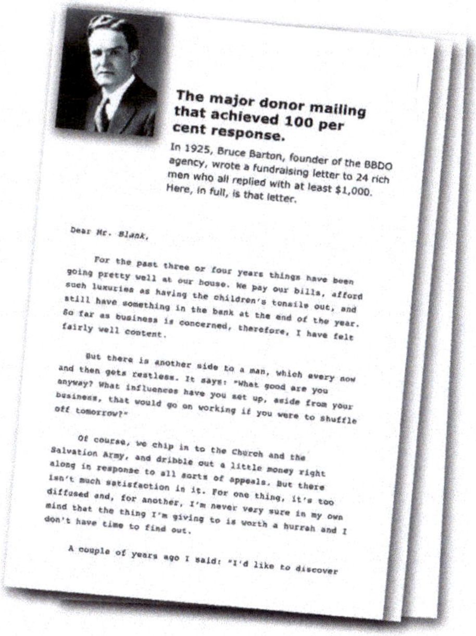

The major donor mailing that achieved 100 per cent response.

In 1925, Bruce Barton, founder of the BBDO agency, wrote a fundraising letter to 24 rich men who all replied with at least $1,000. Here, in full, is that letter.

Dear Mr. Blank,

For the past three or four years things have been going pretty well at our house. We pay our bills, afford such luxuries as having the children's tonsils out, and still have something in the bank at the end of the year. So far as business is concerned, therefore, I have felt fairly well content.

But there is another side to a man, which every now and then gets restless. It says: "What good are you anyway? What influences have you set up, aside from your business, that would go on working if you were to shuffle off tomorrow?"

Of course, we chip in to the Church and the Salvation Army, and dribble out a little money right along in response to all sorts of appeals. But there isn't much satisfaction in it. For one thing, it's too diffused and, for another, I'm never very sure in my own mind that the thing I'm giving to is worth a hurrah and I don't have time to find out.

A couple of years ago I said: "I'd like to discover

IMPACT, INFLUENCE AND OPPORTUNITIES

These and other campaigns from this era shaped fundraising. Their influence is still felt, and the lessons from their experience are still worth sharing. Gifted amateur fundraising writers such as Bruce Barton could still show the professionals a thing or two. The realisation that Live Aid (such a gem it's given its own pages, overleaf) was conceived and carried out entirely by amateur yet instinctive campaigning fundraisers should give the professional fundraising sector pause for thought.

LINKS TO MORE ON 20TH CENTURY FUNDRAISING

https://sofii.org/article/how-the-suffragettes-became-one-of-the-most-successful-brands-ever

https://sofii.org/case-study/british-red-cross-the-7.7-billion-appeal-that-changed-british-fundraising-forever

https://sofii.org/case-study/the-bruce-barton-letter-the-classic-long-copy-letter-from-1925-that-pulled-a-100-per-cent-response

12 Fundraising for massive social change: the Live Aid concerts

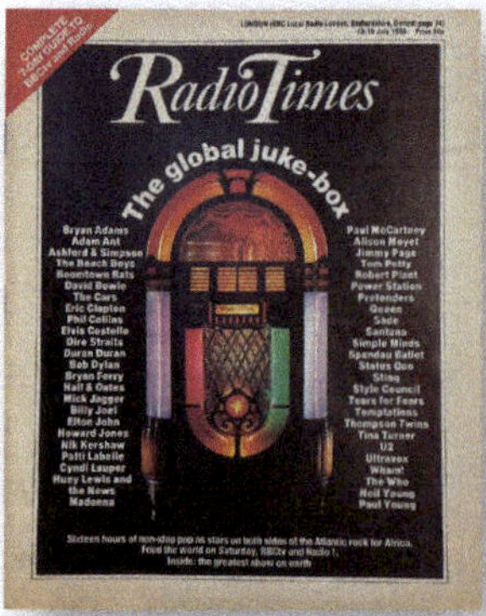

WHY I CHOSE THIS

Conceived to relieve the horror of persistent famine in East Africa, the Live Aid concerts in 1985 weren't just the largest broadcast ever with an estimated live audience of 1.9 billion across 150 nations, it was also an ongoing music-based fundraising extravaganza, a 'global jukebox' that inspired simultaneous events in the UK, USA, Soviet Union, Canada, Japan, Yugoslavia, Austria, Australia and West Germany.[1]

ORIGINS AND OBJECTIVES

Like so many great campaigning fundraising initiatives this international mega-event grew out of a sense of outrage at a wrong that needed righting. The introductory words from the broadcaster who kicked off the spectacle were, 'It's 12 noon in London, 7.00 am in Philadelphia and around the world it's time for Live Aid.' Events fundraising would never be the same again. The line-up included just about every significant band and solo artist. If you didn't appear at Live Aid, you didn't figure.

SIGNIFICANCE AND SPECIAL CHARACTERISTICS

Live Aid also arguably put humanitarian concern at the centre of foreign policy for Western governments. Bob Geldof put it superbly when he said,

1 Source: Wikipedia.

'We took an issue that was nowhere on the political agenda and, through the *lingua franca* of the planet – which is not English but rock 'n' roll – we were able to address the intellectual absurdity and the moral repulsion of people dying of want in a world of surplus.' It also raised an estimated £150 million, with not a professional fundraiser in sight.

BACKGROUND STORY

The Live Aid concerts were conceived as a follow-up to the successful charity single *Do they know it's Christmas*, initiated by rock stars Bob Geldof and Midge Ure. The original idea came from Boy George. But it was Geldof's extraordinary power of peer-to-peer influence through all stages of the event that made it such a phenomenon, right up to the point where he told viewers across the world, 'Don't go to the pub, stay in and give us your fucking money.' (Though this near perfect comment attributed to Geldof came in at No 5 in a survey of people's most memorable TV moments, what he actually said, as verified by TV footage, [2] didn't have the expletive – though Geldof did use it live on TV moments later, in a similar but less pithy context. A shame, perhaps. But the story shows false memory syndrome really is a thing, so it's worth guarding against – another good reason for knowing one's history.)

IMPACT, INFLUENCE AND OPPORTUNITIES

Bob Geldof simply decided that, 'the show should be as big as is humanly possible'. It set new standards in collaborative effort and to this day is an object lesson in can-do attitude, thinking big and never accepting no. This was the moment when everyone watching around the planet came together to make a difference. Live Aid should stand as an example to all campaigning fundraisers to show what might be achieved if, like the music world, they could ever come together in a common aim and work together for the common good. Perhaps we could do something similar for climate change, or inequality, or diversity, or (please fill in your own world-changing aspiration, here). See also transformational campaigns, exhibit 27.

LINKS TO MORE ON FUNDRAISING FOR MASSIVE SOCIAL CHANGE

https://sofii.org/case-study/the-history-of-live-aid

https://www.youtube.com/watch?v=t_6SaRWdJMc&lc=UggxoVhqcJWMt3gCoAEC

2 Source: David Hepworth's blog, 20 October 2007.

PART 3

Foundations of fundraising and campaigning

If you're nice to people, they will be nice back, to you. That's hardly rocket science, nor is it even slightly profound. Indeed, it may be too simple to be taken seriously by many, particularly if, like most charities, your organisation needs to raise ever higher sums to meet ever-increasing demands in an environment of ever-increasing competition. Against this background, it appears, even the most seemingly apparent simple truths can easily be lost. In our working lives, common sense often seems not common at all. The simplest of truths can easily elude our leaders. Our organisations and our supporters pay a heavy price when they do.

Recent experience has led to much re-evaluation and reassessment of how fundraising should be done if it's to deliver maximum value both to donors and the causes that they wish to thrive. In the UK from 2015 to 2017 a complete overhaul of fundraising best practices was attempted by a pop-up organisation called the Commission on the Donor Experience (CDE). CDE was the product of more than 2,000 volunteers from the fundraising community in the UK and worldwide, coming together to heal fundraising and make it better for all. The work CDE started is still ongoing (see exhibit 22) but has already resulted in a transformation in how funds are raised and how fundraisers approach their work. The Supporter Experience Project led by the UK's Chartered Institute of Fundraising is now stimulating further changes designed to enrich the experience of charity supporters and enhance the benefits they enjoy when supporting their chosen causes.

This section features a range of immutable strengths and individual qualities that should characterise the new era of responsible fundraising. They underpin the simple truths that all fundraising has to be built upon clear principles and now, every campaigning fundraiser can join the movement to make fundraising better.

13 Integrity: essential for building trust and confidence

WHY I CHOSE THIS

Integrity is indispensable for a would-be campaigning fundraiser because unshakeable trust and confidence are prerequisites in anyone willing to embark upon the journey to become a committed donor. That trust and confidence has to be rooted in clear, shared, evidently practised principles. Obvious, right? And which area of business would our publics be most entitled to assume will be guided by firm, pure principles and practices? The 'for-change' charity sector, surely? Well, not obviously, as it happens. In fact, maybe, quite wrong.

ORIGINS AND OBJECTIVES

If you had studied the malpractices revealed in the seemingly endless shock-horror exposés of bad or inept fundraising that thronged the pages of the UK media from 2015 to 2017 and beyond, you'd have found that invariably at the root of each transgression was an absence of basic integrity. While preparing for an article on the theme at the time I found the definition below and, as it seemed apt, I rushed to include it. But the little credit at the bottom of the pic irritated me, so I started to trim it off, to discard it.

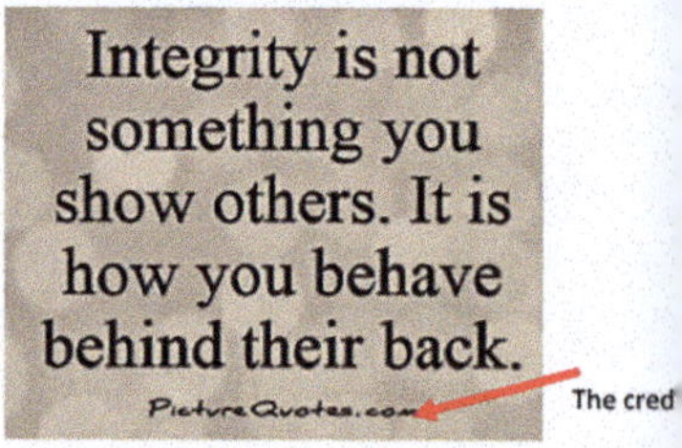

Then I realised what I was doing. How easy it is to jettison integrity for expediency. I hastily reinstated the credit. And learned a lesson in the process.

SIGNIFICANCE AND SPECIAL CHARACTERISTICS

Unless we specifically guard against them, lapses in integrity can strike whenever we're confused by competing priorities such as urgent targets, reports to trustees and the relentless pressure for growth.

BACKGROUND STORY

Shortly before the media storm in 2015 I had lunch with a leading director of fundraising at a top UK charity – someone I admire a lot. During lunch he let fall a remark that stopped me in my tracks. He said, 'We are factory fundraising on an industrial scale.' He wasn't boasting, just stating what he saw as an evident fact. That was the business they were in. Some months later, in the wake of new requirements to break up that apparent paradigm and new regulations imposed to ensure compliance, that same fundraising director said to me, 'My job now is managing decline.'

Unquestionably the pressure for growth and the dominance of targets had led to a culture in many organisations that could be categorised as the voracious, relentless quest for donors' cash, aggressively pursued with at times scant consideration of the impact such a policy was having on donors and non-donors alike. That impact was clearly if not always entirely accurately articulated by all sectors of the British media, at dinner table conversations and in pubs and clubs up and down the land, wherever people met. Yet still some fundraisers sought to deny it, blaming instead a hostile, careless, anti-fundraising Press.

IMPACT, INFLUENCE AND OPPORTUNITIES

Suddenly in fundraising the talk was about principles. Incredible! If this could be captured the potential for change across the sector would be seismic. So, those 2,000 volunteer enthusiasts for good fundraising came together to capture it (see exhibit 22).

Just imagine the transformation that would spring from a renewed commitment to fundamental principles such as integrity, consideration, respect and the proud assertion that pressure, persistence and undue persuasion are not the right approaches for fundraisers. Sure, some deny our need to tackle this because there's evidence many donors will continue to give however inappropriately they've been asked. Campaigning fundraisers must not accept this. Ours should be the business area with the highest integrity, because that's essential to underpin our greatest asset – unshakeable public trust and confidence. If we gain and can keep a rock-solid reputation for this, everything will change. And similar media assaults will in future be impossible.

LINKS TO MORE ON THE IMPORTANCE OF INTEGRITY

https://sofii.org/article/the-6ps-a-blueprint-for-transforming-fundraising-for-good

https://sofii.org/article/the-ken-burnett-archives-integrity

HOW THE AGITATOR SEES IT:

http://agitator.thedonorvoice.com/why-trust-matters-in-fundraising-and-what-to-do-about-it

14 More guiding principles: safety, diversity, morality and the role of trustees

WHY I CHOSE THIS

Trustees, collectively, have the overall legal responsibility for a charity, for its guidance and governance (see also exhibit 50).

* In law, trustees have 'control over, and legal responsibility for, a charity's management and administration', they 'must make sure that the charity is carrying out the purposes for which it is set up, and no other purpose'.
* Trustees' 'duty of prudence' means they 'must make sure the charity's assets are only used to support or carry out its purposes and avoid exposing the charity's assets, beneficiaries or reputation to undue risk'.[1]

The board of trustees, collectively and as individuals, can add great value. Or they can hold the charity back. Quite frequently, they do both.

ORIGINS AND OBJECTIVES

There can be some differences in different countries, of course, notably the USA, but depending on the size and capacity of the charity, generally boards concern themselves with governance and big picture issues, delegating day-to-day executive responsibility to the senior management team. That delegation has to be formally agreed and recorded and the ultimate legal duty of control will always remain with the trustees, not their employees. In small charities the trustees may have executive responsibilities also, but preferably the CEO and his or her colleagues will be separately accountable for the running of the business and the trustees will operate as a parallel, supportive board, mainly offering oversight. The CEO of a charitable company is not a company director in the usual sense – and cannot be a trustee/director.

A good trustee board should consistently provide its charity with wise guidance and support that, were it a commercial business, it could never hope to afford. That trustees should set standards and seek always to do the right thing, is self-evident. Safety, diversity and morality matter, no doubt, yet they can easily be areas that trustees overlook. Because of its dependence on public trust and confidence, the for-change sector should be a paragon of justice, fairness, equality, honesty, integrity and morality. Yet, expensively, the evidence for scrupulous strength and probity in such issues is often depressingly slim.

1 From *The Essential Trustee: what you need to know, what you need to do*, published by the UK Charity Commission.

SIGNIFICANCE AND SPECIAL CHARACTERISTICS

In the wake of the #MeToo movement, Black Lives Matter, #Charitysowhite and other responses to thankfully growing societal intolerance of traditional power abuses, it's been particularly shocking for many to find that the charity sector is not exempt from criticism on such issues – far from it.

BACKGROUND STORY

The two examples cited below illustrate the point. In 2018 an article from leading UK campaigner for better fundraising Giles Pegram CBE (see link below) shone a light on the previously all-but-unreported issue of donors abusing their relationship with fundraisers. And worse, fundraising leadership tolerating that abuse in the interests of securing and preserving donations. The feedback to these articles was frankly terrifying as dozens of fundraisers confessed their harrowing personal tales of abuse while at work. Clearly such concerns must now be front of mind for fundraising leaders.

Diversity is a huge issue for our sector, particularly the (now improving) limited gender balance in senior roles and the still all-too-evident preponderance of charity boards dominated by privileged white males. From 1998 to 2003 I served as chair of trustees at ActionAid, the pinnacle of 13 years as a volunteer member of their international board. I was lucky enough to work then with Salil Shetty, ActionAid's first non-British CEO, an inspired appointment by a board determined to change. Together with Salil and ActionAid's senior management team the board set about rebuilding itself to achieve genuine gender balance among the trustees as well as representation from suitably qualified people from many of the countries where ActionAid works. It proved to be a transformational journey.

'Commitment to diversity is a basic essential of good governance so not-for-profit organisations, one might expect, should have diversity policies and practices deeply embedded at their core. The international anti-poverty charity ActionAid has always been emotionally committed to diversity. It was just, at times, rather difficult to see it in practice, either from the outside looking in or from the inside, looking around. Equally ActionAid was always committed to gender equity and to gender balance at all levels, in all things. Only, that too was often hard to spot. For sure, hearts at ActionAid were in the right places and all intentions

were just as they should be, but in the past the reality was often far from what it should have been.'

From the introduction to *ActionAid's journey to diversity*, see link below

IMPACT, INFLUENCE AND OPPORTUNITIES

Too often in charities the trustee board is seen as an authoritarian, immovable barrier to change. Invariably at conferences around the world fundraisers cite difficulties caused by a blinkered and unreceptive board. It's one of the biggest, most intransigent problems fundraisers face. But change can come and recognition that it's urgently needed is usually the first step. As with clear principles, genuine equity and transparent integrity, true diversity dramatically improves organisational decision-making, levels of debate, staff and volunteer morale, organisational performance and how the organisation is viewed both internally and externally. Expect the change to be resisted, but don't ever give an inch. It's the only way forward and when you get it right, the benefits are immense.

ActionAid's journey to diversity called for substantial investment to ensure sufficient quality applicants could be considered, from all round the world. After decades of paying little more than local travel costs and for indifferent sandwich lunches at trustee meetings, the charity's investment in governance grew hugely to cover international travel and accommodation for trustees coming from the likes of Ghana, Guatemala, Italy, Greece, Brazil, India, Uganda and Malawi. So, no small step, but an investment hugely and demonstrably worth making. At last and proudly, ActionAid could transform into a truly international organisation, living its principles. Since 2003, when my time as chair of trustees at ActionAid ended, all three successive chairs have been African women.

LINKS TO MORE ON GUIDING PRINCIPLES

https://fundraising.co.uk/2018/04/05/unacceptable-behaviour-donors-condoned-charities-things-must-change/

https://sofii.org/article/actionaids-journey-to-diversity

https://sofii.org/article/the-use-and-misuse-of-emotion-section-5-the-creative-use-of-emotion

HOW THE AGITATOR SEES IT:

http://agitator.thedonorvoice.com/lousy-boards-barriers-to-growth-part-3

15 Finding your 'WHY?': why it matters so much

WHY I CHOSE THIS

It's crucial to really understand and define why your supporters support you, and what that means to them. Yet many organisations don't approach this formally, collectively, so have no common, shared understanding of their 'WHY?' Organisations seem to spend endless time and energy on identifying their mission, vision and values but so often these essentials are built upon what the organisation and its officers believe donors *should* be interested in, which isn't necessarily the same thing as what donors *might* be inspired by. The WHY? defines the organisation's appeal and purpose entirely from the donor's viewpoint, which of course is why an appreciation of your donors' WHY? is so much more useful and powerful than any definition of your organisation's mission, vision and values.

'He who has a "why" to live by can bear with almost any "how".'
Friedrich Nietzsche

ORIGINS AND OBJECTIVES

Two charts in a format initially devised by Craig Linton and Paul Stein in their book *Donors for Life*, neatly illustrate the usefulness of this concept. They placed the WHY? at the centre, which of course it is, from the donor's perspective, then built their key relationship development interactions around that. Great storytelling draws potential donors in, helping them to see if the cause is right for them. This leads to multiple opportunities for relationship building, after which asking properly comes naturally and comfortably so the right people can be asked for the right things in the right way and at the right time. Appropriately tailored donor communications create many possibilities for donor care and even donor magic. Informed by this, the process can then be refined and improved as the relationship builds. Soon as I saw Craig and Paul's original, I adapted the style to show recommended practice when placing the donor experience at the centre (from the organisation's point of view) then surrounding that with how donors should experience the charity's key relationship-building aspirations. Both approaches work well for the new age of responsible fundraising.

© Craig Linton/Paul Stein The White Lion Press Limited
Donors for Life: a practitioner's guide to relationship fundraising

While undoubtedly indispensable for fundraisers, storytelling can be a doubled edged sword – as Mark Phillips has observed, other people's stories can bore the hell out of people. Storytelling works best, in Mark's view, when the donor has a rewarding story to tell – to themselves or to others. So, if the fundraiser wishes to spark some storytelling, it'll pay if she or he knows how to do it well.

SIGNIFICANCE AND SPECIAL CHARACTERISTICS

Both the WHY? and the donor experience should be constantly, firmly at the centre of your communications with donors. Just to be provocative we could run a similar chart alongside these two, with 'Ask for more' in the centre and similar boxes menacingly and relentlessly surrounding the centre with messages such as 'ask again', 'upgrade', 'ask for a legacy', 'ask more persistently' and 'ask yet again'. I hope by now you're saying, 'Ah, no – that would illustrate what not to do, wouldn't it? That would all be entirely from the organisation's view.' Good for you! The realisation though is far from universal. It's the paradigm fundraisers everywhere now need to change.

WHAT THE FUNDRAISING CUSTOMER EXPERIENCE SHOULD LOOK LIKE

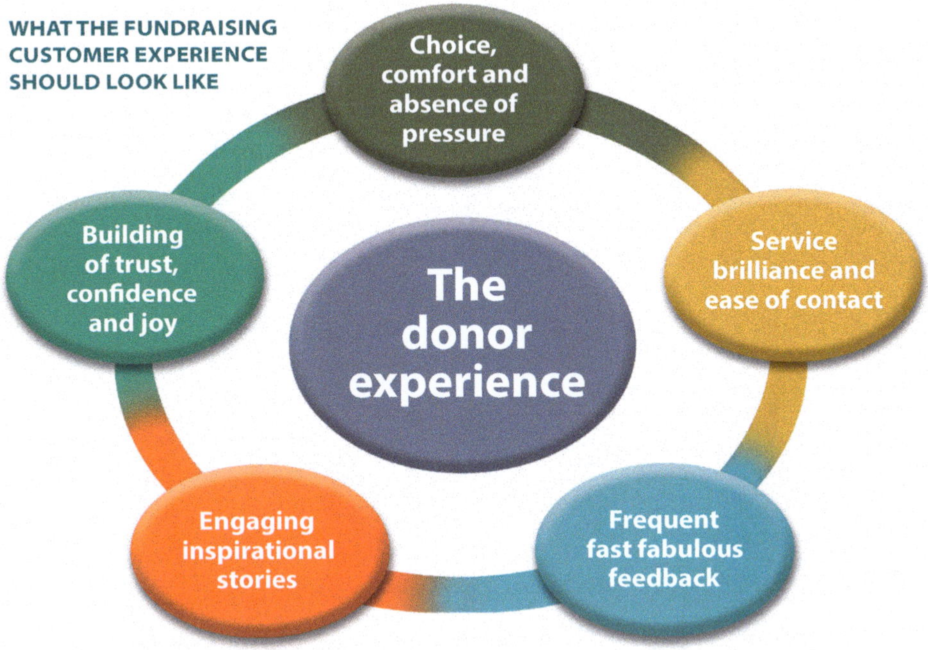

© Ken Burnett 2020

BACKGROUND STORY

Organisations need to work collaboratively to define their WHY? – or rather, their donors' WHY? – and to regularly revisit their definition to keep it fresh and current as well as understood and enthused about by all. For many years my then business partner Alan Clayton and I ran a three-day residential course on emotional fundraising. We always devoted an exceptional amount of the available time to helping participating organisations to find their WHY? There was often resistance to this and at times people found the process difficult, but invariably the time was well spent, though often surprising and even transformational.

Your donors' WHY? for supporting your cause is your holy grail. It is what glues them to your cause and, in time if you treat them well, to your organisation.

But donors may have different WHYs or different degrees to their WHY?– 'I've survived cancer and want others to have the help I've had; I've lost someone to cancer, I want doctors to be able to spot problems earlier; my mum supported a cancer cause all her life and I want to remember her through a gift in her memory/a gift in my will'. And so on.

These need to be grouped under an overarching donor WHY? that unites all those WHYs. As Karin Weatherup explains, if you can capture the next layer down of WHYs, getting closer to that individual's unique experience, you have rocket fuel. You can then make your communications all about them – or so it will feel.

IMPACT, INFLUENCE AND OPPORTUNITIES

Once your fundraising and campaigning teams have a clear understanding of their WHY?, just stand back and watch them work their magic.

LINKS TO MORE ON FINDING YOUR WHY?

https://sofii.org/article/a-practical-evidence-based-guide-thatll-keep-your-relationship-fundraising-on-track

https://sofii.org/article/inspiration-is-scary

HOW THE AGITATOR SEES IT:

http://agitator.thedonorvoice.com/how-do-you-find-out-why-people-give

16 An attitude of gratitude: the priceless art and craft of 'Thankology'

WHY I CHOSE THIS

Something else we were all taught from mother's knee is to always say thank you, promptly, nicely and whenever it's appropriate (like, whenever you get a gift, of any kind). Donors in the recent past must have wondered how on earth such basic politeness (not to mention wisdom) could have become so lost. But all that's changing now as campaigning fundraisers everywhere realise thanking is no tedious fundraising chore, it's one of the best routes to retaining donors long-term and one of the best relationship development opportunities of them all.

> **'Expressing gratitude is a powerful act of civility benefitting both expressers and recipients.'**
>
> Amit Kumar and Nicholas Epley, researchers, University of Chicago

ORIGINS AND OBJECTIVES, SIGNIFICANCE AND SPECIAL CHARACTERISTICS

Sometime in the last ten years or so American copywriter Lisa Sargent invented the concept of Thankology – the art and craft of saying thank you properly, effectively and wisely. Wisely because saying thank you can be solid gold for any young fundraising tyro. It's particularly worth investing in saying thank you properly if you would seek to secure the vital second gift, the one beyond that first 'toe-in-the-water' tester, the gift that leads towards that pinnacle of fundraising aspiration, a regular donation from a committed donor.

> **'You're always thanking donors – but as a donor, without your hard work and dedication my money is worth nothing. It's only money, you guys translate it into love.'**
>
> Letter from Clara, a real-life donor who has confirmed a legacy pledge in her will. From *Thankology: a fundraiser's guide to keeping your donors longer, and giving stronger, through gratitude*, by Lisa Sargent, to be published end 2021

BACKGROUND STORY

When I started out in fundraising the process of saying thank you – or the sending of a (usually drab and dull) receipt – was more observed in its omission than in its practice. Thank-you letters were almost always sent way too late, were hastily written and uninspiring, reflecting the enthusiasm with which they were sent. More than just a chore, its sending was considered unnecessary by many, a barely justifiable expense at least for mid- to low-value donors. Some charities even had policies of not thanking donors who gave below a certain level (so these un-thanked donors would often go on to leave their worldly goods, house, cash and jewellery to another, more polite cause). Even major donors often failed to get an appropriate acknowledgment of sometimes four-figure gifts, and many complain (usually to their rich friends) that they still do. Why should anyone give anything if the recipient can't be bothered to confirm safe receipt, far less their appreciation?

THANK YOU

IMPACT, INFLUENCE AND OPPORTUNITIES

Lisa Sargent's Thank-you Clinics are the most visited area of SOFII.org, the Showcase of Fundraising Innovation and Inspiration, bar none, with many hundreds of thousands of visits over the years. Readers particularly love the free real-life annotated before and after rewrites that people can learn from and pinch. To see why people so love being thanked properly, have a look at the ad from Toronto Dominion Bank, linked below. Saying thank you isn't the only way of approaching the basic politeness of properly acknowledging a freely given gift. You can also congratulate, say well done, you've done something significant. There's a lot to this seemingly simple act, so much that Lisa has written a book about it. Those who wish to prosper will do well to pay it good heed, not least for its many lessons on the powerful role that an attitude of gratitude, when properly managed, can play in donor retention – perhaps the biggest challenge facing the for-change sector everywhere – and in delivering lifetime value both to donors and the causes they support.

'I know without a doubt how thanking donors works a special kind of magic on retention and revenues.'

From *Thankology: a fundraiser's guide to keeping your donors longer, and giving stronger, through gratitude*, by Lisa Sargent, to be published end 2021

A thank you can truly make someone's day, as Toronto Dominion Bank shows so entertainingly. Not for the first time, it's evidence that charities can learn from their commercial cousins.

Campaigning fundraisers need to work at their thankology – to think like a thankologist. It will repay them big time as, better than anything else we might do, it will enable donors to see that they are seen, that their role in this great work is recognised and valued. How to do this is within easy reach and almost certainly fundraisers will come to enjoy it as they realise that showing appreciation is almost as satisfying as giving itself. Generosity is not just reciprocal, it's infectious. By thanking creatively and developing an attitude of gratitude, campaigning fundraisers can influence, even channel this infectiousness, provided they can encourage and learn to trust their donors' potential to enjoy and spread the joy and benefits of giving, at a pace that suits them.

LINKS TO MORE ON AN ATTITUDE OF GRATITUDE

https://sofii.org/article/how-to-write-a-better-thank-you-letter-and-why-it-matters

https://sofii.org/case-study/toronto-dominion-charitable-trust-tdthanksyou-video

https://sofii.org/article/welcome-to-the-art-and-science-of-positive-thanking

https://sofii.org/article/a-simple-equation-plus-three-big-reasons-to-buy-this-book

HOW THE AGITATOR SEES IT:

https://agitator.thedonorvoice.com/the-high-cost-of-undervaluing-gratitude

Thank you!

Thank you! Thank you!

ChildVision

National Education Centre for Blind Children

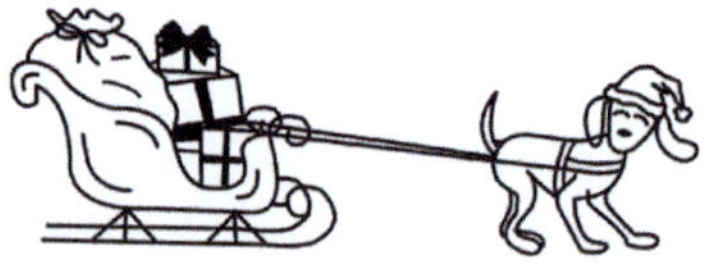

Mrs E. N. Murphy
The High Street
Anytown
Ireland

30th June,

Dear Mrs Murphy,

Second star to the right, and straight on till morning.

Your Christmas donation of €70.00 has given our disabled blind children wings to fly here at ChildVision. 1

Teaching toys... therapy toys... triumphant toys. The magic of music... magnificent, miraculous, mobility horses. Braille books to bring bold, bright beginnings. Dazzling adaptive technology to spark independence in a sighted world.

Gifts of a lifetime, all. And all thanks to you.

Here at ChildVision you are the song in our hearts and the star in our sky. We couldn't help disabled blind children in Ireland, without you. Thank you so very much for caring this Christmas.

Please know that you are always welcome to call us on 01 837 3635 with any queries you have. We are happy to help you however we can.

Here's to a new year filled with love, learning, and laughter,

Brian Allen

Brian Allen
CEO, ChildVision

P.S. Unless you've requested otherwise, I'll write you again in the months ahead to up date you on how your generosity is touching the lives of the children here – watch for your ChildVision Member Newsletter coming in spring. Until then, in return for the great love you have shown to Ireland's disabled blind children, thank you. And may all your wishes come true this year.

ChildVision, Grace Park Road, Drumcondra, Dublin 9
T 01 837 3635 E info@ChildVision.ie W www.ChildVision.ie

Directors: Shane Cowley (Chairperson), David Myers, Monica Leech, Dan Browne, Michael O'Shea, Christopher Cassedy, Josephs O'Reilly, Michael Monaghan, Richard Ryan, Marian Harte
Registered in Dublin, No 453711, CHY817

A generous response to a generous act. Child Vision nails it with this fine example of a sincere and thoughtful thank-you letter. Courtesy of Lisa Sargent, *Thankology*.

17 Essential reading: the great fundraiser's bookshelf

WHY I CHOSE THIS

People are often defined by the books that line their shelves. I've always hoped that books I've written would not sit languishing on, or decorating, any fundraiser's bookshelf but rather should be by her or his side, open on the desk, well-thumbed, a constant support and source of reference and inspiration. No doubt, there's a vast and valuable resource in the growing body of books written specifically for fundraisers.

ORIGINS AND OBJECTIVES, SIGNIFICANCE AND SPECIAL CHARACTERISTICS

Recently the SOFII website mobilised its supporters around the world to compile a library of the best, most recommended books. Before long there were 195 good books nominated in the first attempt alone. We could easily add more. Of course, despite the richness of their content, few will own or actually read more than a fraction of these. They will be the real enthusiasts, the real winners. So, for this collection I've selected just three books to celebrate, as indicative of a vast, incalculably valuable resource. And, what a difficult choice!

BACKGROUND STORIES

- David Ogilvy's *Ogilvy on Advertising* has guided successive generations of would-be effective advertisers through acres of experience-based wise sayings and instructive anecdotes, from the days when advertising was an interesting and informative part of our lives. Like countless others I modelled the best years of my business life on the sayings of David Ogilvy and prospered as a direct result.
- Mal Warwick's *Revolution in the Mailbox* is described as, 'how to really understand fundraising's reigning big idea, direct mail – the arcane mix of art and science that creates a wonderful postal relationship between charity and donor'. Again, it's based on a long life of hands-on learning, is a great read and sparks lessons constantly.
- Penelope Burk's *Donor-Centred Leadership: what it takes to build a high-*

performance fundraising team would be my third choice, though its precursor, *Donor-Centred Fundraising,* wouldn't be far behind. I particularly liked that book because the research it reported on proved the basis of the theory I'd put forward in *Relationship Fundraising* a few years earlier. This book is also based on solid research and practical guidance for donor-focused campaigning fundraisers, with a cornucopia of rich ideas for building a great fundraising environment in which talent and enthusiasm can thrive.

IMPACT, INFLUENCE AND OPPORTUNITIES

Some books have been significantly more impactful and influential in this field than others. It would be invidious of me to comment further, so I won't. The common characteristics of the very best business books are that they're well written as well as perceptive, well-structured and researched, so they're a compelling, easy read that effortlessly instils fresh knowledge and insights in a comfortable, accessible way. There should I'm sure be a similar catalogue of talking books and even short 'how to' videos. Hopefully, something SOFII can stretch to in the not-too-distant future.

LINKS TO MORE ESSENTIAL READING

https://sofii.org/article/the-great-fundraisers-bookshelf

https://sofii.org/article/david-ogilvy-a-profile-of-the-father-of-advertising

https://sofii.org/article/how-to-really-understand-fundraisings-reigning-big-idea-direct-mail

https://sofii.org/article/could-this-be-the-sea-change-that-fundraising-really-needs

HOW THE AGITATOR SEES IT:

http://agitator.thedonorvoice.com/the-loss-of-an-exceptional-friend-of-fundraising

18 Spending time with the masters: learning from the leading lights

WHY I CHOSE THIS

Every field of endeavour has its gurus, its sages, its teachers and most have their rogues and charlatans too, so it pays to be careful. Because of the breadth and depth of subjects that fundraising campaigners need to master, it's sound sense to develop a ready familiarity with wise and experienced communicators from a wide variety of fields. Though the list is long, some of my favourites are summarised here.

> **'One day a man walked into a London agency and asked to see the boss. He had bought a country house and was about to open it as a hotel. Could the agency help him to get customers? He had $500 to spend. Not surprisingly, the head of the agency turned him over to the office boy, who happened to be the author of this book. I invested his money in penny postcards and mailed them to well-heeled people living in the neighbourhood. Six weeks later the hotel opened to a full house. I had tasted blood.'**
>
> David Ogilvy, *Ogilvy on Advertising*, 1985

ORIGINS AND OBJECTIVES

Some sages, such as Ogilvy, are born with it, they have a natural magic touch. But even for them, mostly wisdom is acquired from long years of experience, testing, trial and error. So for sure the true sages can give you a shortcut or two, or at least a hand up. Campaigning fundraisers need to familiarise themselves with the wisdom of the world of advertising, response marketing, communications, psychology, demographics, behavioural economics, general and event management, leadership and a range of other specialisms. Fortunately, there are plenty of sages that repay study: the challenge is to identify those most worth listening to.

SIGNIFICANCE AND SPECIAL CHARACTERISTICS

One inevitability of this age of information overload and the worldwide web is that there's simply so much good stuff around – how is the keen new recruit to find just the essence of what matters most? Well, this is where a trusted source that will do the work for you comes into its own.

BACKGROUND STORY

There are too many wise advisers to mention, of course, but a bit of name-dropping here might be useful, if I mention a few of those particular to the would-be campaigning fundraiser. Other than those previously mentioned masters referenced elsewhere in this book I urge fundraisers to spend some time with the collected writings of George Smith, Mal Warwick, Roger Craver, Penelope Burk, Harvey McKinnon, Kay Sprinkel Grace, Judith Nichols, Giles Pegram, Pamela Grow, Nancy Schwarz, Colin Wheildon, Peter Drucker, Seth Godin (plus others outside the fundraising field, too numerous to mention), Erica Waasdorp, Bruce Barton, Tom Ahern, Drayton Bird, John Watson, Jerry Huntsinger, Jennie Thompson, Lisa Sargent, Nick Allen, David Love, Stephen Pidgeon, Stephen Thomas, Mark Phillips, John Lepp, Alan Clayton, Sean Triner, Fiona McPhee, Gavin Coopey, Leo Orland and... well, apologies to anyone I've left out who should be included. Campaigning fundraisers are lucky to have ready access to a glittering array of great mentors. Just recognising this will catapult your career forward.

It also helps if you love what you do, read a lot (see exhibit 17) – the right kind of things of course – take time to sit still and meditate, listen to music, study nature, travel, try new things, break out of your bubble, challenge the ideas of others, push the boundaries, spend quality time with children and old people, learn to observe and to listen, talk to strangers, develop your creativity in multiple areas and do the washing up or similar household chores both regularly and well. Master that lot and success will be easy.

Get out and meet the people that matter. These days most of our interactions are virtual. We're required to be comfortable with multiple online technologies, to debate, present and network virtually. It can be difficult to inspire and inform when you are simply a cheery face framed within a minute, though colourful, rectangle. But it's not impossible.

IMPACT, INFLUENCE AND OPPORTUNITIES

Wise words from these sages down the ages have cemented many a career's foundations and have often led to great rewards, to spectacular business successes, or at least to recurring lightbulb moments and inspiration. I've recorded my debt to the great Ogilvy, whose insightful musings directly helped me to launch the first advertising, marketing and communications agency in Europe specialising in the for-change sector. 'Helped' really doesn't do justice to his contribution. His insights and guidance propelled and enriched me.

> **'Knowledge is a process of piling up facts; wisdom lies in their simplification.'**
>
> Martin H Fischer, painter, author and professor of physiology

The opportunities to be found in the sayings of the acknowledged masters are as numerous as the stars. And as filled with potential.

LINKS TO MORE ON SPENDING TIME WITH THE MASTERS

https://sofii.org/article/david-ogilvy-a-profile-of-the-father-of-advertising
https://sofii.org/article/david-ogilvys-secret-weapon

HOW THE AGITATOR SEES IT:

http://agitator.thedonorvoice.com/my-pantheon-of-fundraising-curmudgeons

19 The easy convenience of regular giving: ActionAid, Plan, Dogs Trust and others

WHY I CHOSE THIS

For most people £10.00 per month is much easier to afford than £100.00 per annum, despite the latter costing a lot less. It's what the mail order business calls, 'easy payments'. Marry this with automatic fund collection (also known as EFT, autogiro or direct debit), add in the wonder-force that is inertia and you have the magic formula that fuels most successful fundraising organisations. My earliest professional fundraising success rested upon recruiting and developing mostly monthly donors for the charity ActionAid. So successful was ActionAid with this simple recruitment proposition for building their donor files that in a few short years it came from nowhere to be one of the top 20 UK fundraising charities. This experience laid the foundations for my understanding of what campaigning fundraisers should be offering their donors.

ORIGINS AND OBJECTIVES

'Mony a mickle maks a muckle.'
Ancient Scots saying, perhaps by Robbie Burns

Burns' observation above, loosely translated, means a lot of small things add up to something big. It's the essence of charity fundraising. Monthly giving makes sense for both fundraising organisations and their donors. Most people are paid monthly. Pensions and dividends arrive each month. Payments that coincide with income really suit people. Charities want steady, regular, reliable income. Not for nothing do they refer to their regular donors as 'committed', but it's a commitment often underpinned by the powerful hold of inertia, which inhibits cancellation.

Monthly donors stay longer, their predictability aids confidence and future planning and it's simple, affordable and convenient for donors. It should be a wonderful experience too. Tax recovery schemes such as GiftAid are much more willingly taken up by regular donors. And banking systems that facilitate electronic funds transfer make the process much easier, safer and more forgettable also. Plus, a large cohort of regular donors brings a multitude of benefits when campaigning, building relationships, identifying major donors, impressing potential new donors and, most significantly, in the fullness of time, in preparing the ground for the ultimate gift – a legacy.

SIGNIFICANCE AND SPECIAL CHARACTERISTICS

Despite its ease and evident rightness, it's only comparatively recently that clued-in fundraisers actively set out to recruit regular monthly donors in volume. The spectacular growth of UK fundraising charities in the 1980s and 90s owed much to the effective promotion of regular giving, as monthly donors were recruited often in their tens of thousands. The other proposition that I latched on to at the time – giving by legacy – has proved a harder stretch to embed both in the charities who offer it and with the public who, we hope, might rally to do it. Yet monthly giving remains the optimum starting point for any legacy campaign. And increasing the take-up of legacies will be the 'philosopher's stone' for fundraisers – the most hopeful prospect of stimulating riches beyond dreams for our causes.

BACKGROUND STORY

The foundation of a truly self-sustaining voluntary organisation is a viable, growing throng of passionately motivated real supporters, all committed, long-term donors who will support your cause down the years, month after month, through thick and thin, then after a lifetime of supporting and donating will ultimately leave their final farewell gift, a legacy. Identifying, inspiring, recruiting and retaining these people is the core function for the modern campaigning fundraiser.

Had I studied history more closely I'd have realised much earlier the provenance and evolution of this transformational idea. As it was, I saw only part of the story. But that was enough. For me the boom in ActionAid's growth in the late 1970s and early 80s through effective direct marketing of its high value monthly giving scheme was enough to make me a lifelong enthusiast for regular giving schemes. So, I added my voice to

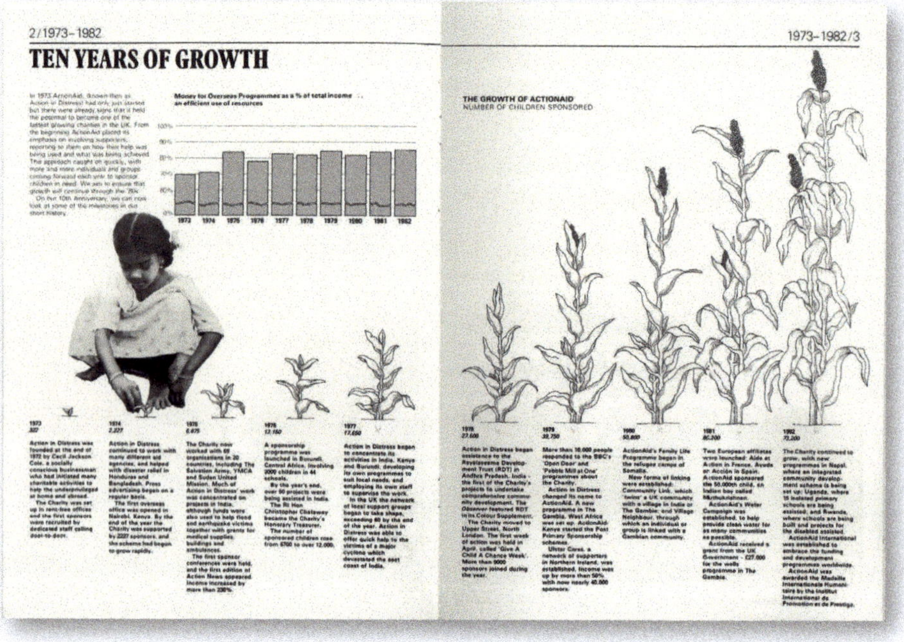

what soon became a chorus advocating the multiple benefits of monthly giving. I made the promotion of monthly giving a central thesis for my 1992 book *Relationship Fundraising: a donor-based approach to the business of raising money*, one of just two prime 'must-do' activities – the second being legacies.

IMPACT, INFLUENCE AND OPPORTUNITIES

The effective promotion of regular monthly giving became a bandwagon and soon everyone was doing it. The basic fundraising paradigm of '£15.00 will save a child's life' soon shifted to '£2.00 per month...' and grew steadily from there. Whether this enthusiasm was always beneficial for or appreciated by the donor classes is a moot point. But for sure it grew fundraising organisations and gave them solid financial foundations.

Monthly giving sponsorship schemes as popularised by ActionAid, Plan, Dogs Trust and others involved a significant monthly donation. Soon, lower value schemes designed to recruit new donors in volume – priced at £2 or £3 per month – became the most common proposition, which made higher value giving harder to secure, as the low ask encouraged donors to believe £3 each month is all that's required. Bluefrog's Mark Phillips points out that research studies into regular giving show interesting phenomena operating in this unusual market. The UK is a mature market and donors who hit a seemingly magic threshold of regular gifts (about 5 or 6) tend to start cancelling older direct debits when they take out a new one. According to Mark, Charities Aid Foundation data show there's a sticking point around 30 to 33 per cent of the population willing to give by direct debit, a percentage that, so far, has shown little propensity to change.

Which is still a huge chunk of the population. And might be an opportunity, if ways can be found to increase it. Direct recruitment to a regular gift isn't the only route. Upgrading from a low initial ask is possible, but difficult. Often a cash gift can be an easier route for donors. Those who've made at least two single donations in a year will often agree to sign up for a regular monthly collection – particularly if the donor is stewarded effectively in a programme that delivers a consistently rewarding experience.

Monthly giving remains the central proposition of most fundraising success stories today and will do going forward. Because it works, splendidly, for both donor and cause. But still, we can get better at it. Income from regular givers, already huge, has the potential to multiply many times if campaigning fundraisers can only get better at consistently providing delightful donor experiences that show the donor benefits too.

LINKS TO MORE ON REGULAR GIVING

https://sofii.org/case-study/actionaid-the-postal-parent-advert
https://sofii.org/case-study/dogs-trust-sponsor-a-dog
https://sofii.org/case-study/the-plan-the-launch-of-child-sponsorship-spain-1937

HOW THE AGITATOR SEES IT:

http://agitator.thedonorvoice.com/great-monthly-giving-is-in-the-details

20 Legacies: the ultimate gift after a lifelong relationship

WHY I CHOSE THIS

As we've just seen in exhibit 19, for good causes the legacy proposition has at least as much income potential as monthly giving, maybe even more, though so far it's proved a harder sell, with disappointingly limited take-up even among regular donors. Which doesn't mean this can't be changed. For centuries legacies and bequests have fuelled charitable activity in many cultures, often providing the donors – who for sure can't take their earthly riches with them – with the deep satisfaction of knowing that their ultimate gift will enable good works to continue long after they, its initiators, have shuffled off this mortal coil. Legacies offer an extension of mortality, even a semblance of immortality. So far, it seems, this message has missed most people.

ORIGINS AND OBJECTIVES

Most of us accept the old cliché, you can't take it with you, so we arrange our affairs to benefit family and friends, perhaps including a bequest to a favourite charity or two in the process. Which is just as it should be, though the percentage of us leaving anything to charity is really very small. Many still don't even consider leaving a gift to a charity in their will, perhaps because the benefits or even the possibilities haven't been adequately or appealingly explained. Those without surviving family tend to leave the biggest bequests to charities, and they're a relatively small part of the total population. They're also most likely to be female, as with couples it's the wives who are the most common last survivor. Yet thanks largely to this small, highly motivated and selfless band, in the UK legacies provide one third of all individual giving. Though it has to be reiterated that, as yet they come from a disappointingly small number of people.

SIGNIFICANCE AND SPECIAL CHARACTERISTICS

We can change that and move giving by legacy from the chorus line to top of the bill; from being a minority interest to being *de rigueur* for every donor.

The gift of a legacy costs a donor nothing in his or her lifetime. It's a way of ensuring there can actually be life after death, because your compassion and your impact can live on long after you have gone, continuing to do good, doing what you want to do to make a difference in a world of trouble. That's an immortality of sorts, the selling of which shouldn't be beyond us.

BACKGROUND STORY

It used to be assumed that legacies fell into a charity's lap like manna from Heaven. Many charities still account separately for legacies, viewing them as windfall, not part of fundraised income. For sure legacies can be promoted, though the concept of legacy marketing – widely discussed and encouraged in charity circles – should perhaps be avoided or at least rethought as many donors, unsurprisingly, find the mere idea troubling, even offensive. But any charity that invests in building its individual donor file and delivering a fine supporter experience will inevitably find, within a surprisingly short time too, that it has also invested in increasing its income from charitable bequests and legacies.

IMPACT, INFLUENCE AND OPPORTUNITIES

Just as it would be hard to overestimate the good that charitable legacies have done and continue to do, it's impossible to exaggerate the additional good they could do if campaigning fundraisers can get just a bit more effective at inspiring more of our donors to take up this simple, sensible, so-easy-to-justify act. As legacy (bequest) giving from a tiny minority of donors already accounts for such a huge chunk of all donations from individuals, it's also hard to overestimate the potential surge in income that charities would enjoy were it possible to finally find a way to make giving by legacy a must-have for all donors.

> **'It's not about death. It's about life.**
> **Often, fundraisers and volunteers say that they don't like talking about gifts in Will because they feel they are talking about death. This, however, is a mistake. Research in the UK has shown that donors who make a gift to charity live longer than those who don't. And if they leave a legacy gift, they live even longer!'**
>
> David Love, *Green Green*, 2020

Leaving a legacy to one's favourite charitable cause or causes should be part of our culture, as British as fish and chips, as French as *la baguette*, as Spanish as tapas, as Italian as pasta, as American as apple pie and as Australian as jolly swagmen. It can be, for sure. A charitable legacy can add happiness, purpose, fulfilment, meaning and satisfaction to far more lives than benefit from the action now. The promotion of a charitable legacy is a truly unique business activity, though perhaps not the easiest – if you're ever tempted to refer to it as legacy marketing, just ask a few donors to tell you what they'd think of their favourite charity doing such a thing. Of course it requires acres of sensitivity and care in spades, but it also offers endless opportunities for creativity and appropriately inspirational communication.

LINKS TO MORE ON LEGACIES

https://sofii.org/article/just-the-facts-on-legacy-giving
https://sofii.org/case-study/wwf-integrated-legacy-marketing-campaign
https://sofii.org/case-study/the-rnli-legacy-letter
https://sofii.org/article/should-you-enthusiastically-promote-legacy-giving-when-people-are-dying?

HOW THE AGITATOR SEES IT:

http://agitator.thedonorvoice.com/dealing-with-doubts-about-legacy-giving-in-the-pandemic-and-depression

21 The science of fundraising: testing to find what works best

WHY I CHOSE THIS

The work campaigning fundraisers do is way too important to be left to chance. Yet experience shows, way too often, left to chance is what it is, because far too often the choices fundraisers have to make are guided by assumption or opinion rather than by experience or the discipline of actual results. Leaving fundraising communication to chance is a choice, not a necessity – not a wise choice at that, though opted for frequently, nonetheless. So, our organisations should encourage and even insist upon rigorous testing and ensure that their fundraisers excel at it.

ORIGINS AND OBJECTIVES

In pursuit of their core obligation to inspire, recruit, retain and develop new and existing donors, fundraisers routinely deploy sizeable expenditure budgets, so they'll spend huge amounts of their donors' money, usually more money than any of them individually will ever spend on anything else in all their life. The imperative to spend that money wisely and cost-effectively should be every fundraiser's abiding obsession. So why are fundraisers so often unfamiliar with the techniques, obligations and benefits of testing?

SIGNIFICANCE AND SPECIAL CHARACTERISTICS

Much has been written on the value and methodology of testing. Two leaders in this field that I recommend for all fundraisers are David Ogilvy and Colin Wheildon. But the leading architects of tested, scientific communication are Claude Hopkins and John Caples. Reviews of their seminal works are linked overleaf.

> **'Only half of my advertising works.
> The trouble is, I don't know which half…'**
>
> Lord Leverhulme, 1851–1925, at the time the world's largest advertiser

So-called 'above the line' advertising types tend to put little emphasis on testing or direct response, preferring to invoke vague, intangible or difficult-to-measure concepts such as image, recognition and brand awareness. Direct marketing types who live and die by their immediate direct results depend entirely upon rigorous testing. So must it be with campaigning fundraisers.

BACKGROUND STORY

In 1977, when I started in fundraising, testing was entirely at the core of the craft and art of direct marketing, which in turn was emerging as the new way forward for fundraisers committed to donor-recruitment and

development. As anyone with any experience then knew, testing was what kept this new and erratic vehicle on its tracks. Yet somehow over the years that central importance and appreciation of testing has markedly declined, not everywhere, but generally. When the subject of testing comes up, if it ever does, a newly recruited fundraiser will most likely look blankly. 'We can't afford that,' she or he might claim. Or she might ask, 'isn't that something the agency does?' Back in the day our lives were ruled by the precious, blessed guard book, safe home for all our expensively collected data and test results. The guard book now seems all but extinct, even though its electronic counterpart could do the job far faster, better and more easily now. It's hard to see how a modern fundraiser can function without it. Badly, I'd guess. Expensively, I assume. But somehow, function without it they do.

IMPACT, INFLUENCE AND OPPORTUNITIES

As advertising is expensive, its results must be measured. According to John Caples a change of headline might result in response increasing by 17 times. Is that worth knowing? Of course it is. Claude Hopkins was the first eminent adman to realise the distinction between image advertising and response. He created the concept of 'reason why' advertising, so promulgated the radical idea that advertising isn't a matter of chance but can be carefully and precisely directed. The key to this is testing. Historical analysis quickly shows that down through the ages it's rigorous, continual testing and refinement of message that underpins most of the consistent growth and success of our nation's great fundraising organisations.

'Advertising agencies waste their client's money repeating the same mistakes. I recently counted 49 advertisements set in reverse type (white type on black background) in one issue of a magazine, long years after research demonstrated that reverse is difficult to read.'

David Ogilvy, *Ogilvy on Advertising*, 1985

Once any promotion is published it's in the public arena and therefore is fair game for anyone to praise or criticise as they see fit. Countering domestic abuse is a great cause, one that deserves the very best care and creativity that campaigning fundraisers can bring. In the early days of the 2020 Covid pandemic an ad ran in the UK national press that was so obviously ignorant of what works in direct response that I and others were able to publicly critique it at conferences as committing at least a dozen different yet instructive errors, all of which would have reduced response. You can only test one thing at a time, of course. But no one trained in the basics of direct response fundraising would make these errors. The trouble is, we see such ads way too often. There is an opportunity to change that. It calls for a culture of rigorous, professional testing and the realisation

A 'clever' ad, with shortcomings

- No humans, no eye contact.
- No proposition, direct or otherwise. No case for support.
- No indication of what a gift will achieve.
- No call to action. Nothing to tell potential donors what to do.
- No contact details.
- No website link. No phone number.
- No coupon (for the address).
- No shopping list.
- No credit card options
- No suggested giving amounts.
- No emotional hook.
- Reversed out type is hard to read.
- Just a bald ask for cash.

that fundraising communication is a skill that can be acquired only by those prepared and equipped to put in the time to do it properly. As David Ogilvy once put it, 'A blind pig can sometimes find truffles, but it helps to know that they are found in oak forests.'

Of course we can learn from failures and turkeys too. See also exhibit 48, for the *Bad Ads* showcase.

LINKS TO MORE ON THE SCIENCE OF FUNDRAISING

https://sofii.org/article/investing-in-testing

https://sofii.org/article/advertisings-earliest-genius-and-how-he-can-help-your-advertisements-to-work-better-predictably

https://sofii.org/article/which-of-our-ads-will-work-best-where-when-and-why

https://sofii.org/article/sorry-but-youre-just-not-my-type

https://sofii.org/article/a-bad-ad-at-a-bad-time

https://sofii.org/article/bring-back-the-indispensable-guard-book

HOW THE AGITATOR SEES IT:

http://agitator.thedonorvoice.com/testing-best-practices-part-1

22 Redefining fundraising: the Commission on the Donor Experience's 28 projects

WHY I CHOSE THIS

This exhibit charts a turning point for UK fundraising. 'Charity fundraising has never been more important... [so it's] particularly crucial that we get fundraising right.' So said Sir Stuart Etherington, chair of the UK government-initiated review into fundraising self-regulation prompted by the public outrage that followed the blitz of shock-horror media exposés of fundraising malpractices between 2015 and 2017 that I mentioned in this book's introduction. The scandal, which all but overwhelmed the UK voluntary sector, was triggered by the suicide of a 92-year-old volunteer poppy-seller, Mrs Olive Cooke. Her story, and the consequent catastrophe, is linked below. This exhibit explains how, belatedly, UK fundraisers responded.

ORIGINS AND OBJECTIVES

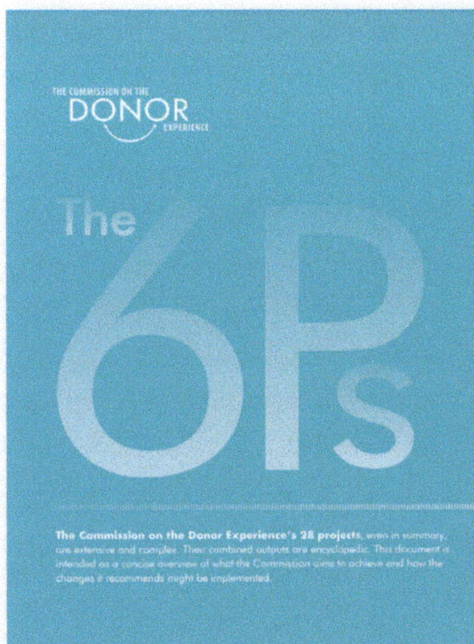

Even before the first critical stories broke it was clear to all but the most blinkered observers that fundraising in Britain was going sadly wrong and major change was overdue. But as is so often the case, Cassandras[1] are mostly ignored and catastrophe has to strike before serious action is taken. Over decades a prevailing preoccupation with ever-increasing financial targets led fundraisers in many charities to focus on raising money in ways often unwelcome to donors and counter-productive to building the kind of relationships and programmes upon which long-term fundraising success depends. In their pursuit of ever more and larger donations to hit ever-growing financial objectives, many fundraising leaders lost sight of what they could and should be doing to deliver, consistently, an exemplary experience for their donors and other supporters.

In response, in July 2015 the Commission on the Donor Experience

1 Cassandra was the soothsayer in ancient Troy cursed to utter true prophecies but never be believed. Towards the end of the siege she wandered the city's streets bewailing impending doom, while most of Troy's citizens decided that this wooden horse they'd found was just the excuse they needed to have a big party. Just saying...

(CDE) was set up: a fundraiser-led initiative that galvanised upwards of 2,000 volunteer fundraisers and others in the UK and around the world to document the theory and best practices of donor-focused fundraising, in the belief that a detailed analysis of it would point to an alternative, better way. Their vision was nothing less than to change the culture of fundraising once and for all, to put the supporter experience at the heart of fundraising practice. On the basis that, if giving is a good experience, donors will do more of it and if it isn't, they'll soon stop, the Commission saw clearly that improving the supporter experience, underpinned by light touch improvements in the system of regulation, would result in substantial growth in fundraising income from happier donors staying longer and giving more, willingly. CDE's first step was to document and evaluate the best of donor-focused practices across 28 individual projects, each focused on a main area of fundraising, each compiled and reviewed by hands-on specialists with expertise in each area.

SIGNIFICANCE AND SPECIAL CHARACTERISTICS

To achieve this cultural transformation CDE called for volunteers to define current understanding of best practices and what organisations needed to change. More than 2,000 people responded to the challenge, from all parts of the voluntary sector, mainly from the UK but also internationally – a massive and unique response to the obvious need to put right what was wrong in fundraising. The CDE initiative set out a framework for a new era of responsible fundraising. Additional to the 28 reports, a major output was the production of *The 6Ps* document (purpose, permanent change, principles, pillars of change, practical actions and promise to donors) which attempted to distil the key lessons from across all 28 CDE projects into an eight-page blueprint for the change that's needed.

BACKGROUND STORY

The CDE concluded that if fundraising charities are to thrive they should transform, permanently, into the most supporter-focused business area of all. Following publication of the Commission's detailed reports and the enthusiasm with which these were received, the UK's Chartered Institute of Fundraising (CIoF) took up the challenge to continue, improve and disseminate understanding of the donor-based approach to the business of raising money, through their Supporter Experience Project. This remains a work in progress.

'The relationship between a charity and its donors has to be cherished and donors must be placed firmly at the heart of fundraising in the future.'

Andrew Hind, former CEO, the Charity Commission, then chair of the Fundraising Standards Board

IMPACT, INFLUENCE AND OPPORTUNITIES

There's a wealth of information in the 28 CDE reports and the CIoF's Supporter Experience Project has already added significantly to this. The challenge is to embed this understanding in individual fundraising organisations, as a core part of their culture. To succeed, this calls for commitment and leadership from senior management teams in every charity across the country.

SOFII's 32 *Lightbulb Moments* are an effort to distil the content of the CDE's voluminous output into a series of easily digestible, bite-sized chunks of what really matters most. The acid test for the initiative though will be in the last of the 6Ps mentioned opposite – a promise to donors that change really has come. Every individual charity should embed at the heart of its DNA the donor-based approach to delivering a consistently good supporter experience. As evidence, it should provide all its constituencies with true accountability by publishing a detailed promise to donors, assuring them that these standards and criteria are firmly, permanently in place. While implementing this across the country should be eminently possible, it won't happen without renewed commitment from campaigning fundraisers everywhere.

LINKS TO MORE ON REDEFINING FUNDRAISING

https://sofii.org/cde/the-commission-on-the-donor-experience

https://sofii.org/cde/the-6ps-a-blueprint-for-transforming-fundraising

https://sofii.org/article/sofiis-letter-to-the-future

https://sofii.org/article/the-olive-cooke-story

HOW THE AGITATOR SEES IT:

http://agitator.thedonorvoice.com/fundraising-evolution-and-revolution

23 *'Where do I start?'*: your first few weeks as a campaigning fundraiser

WHY I CHOSE THIS

Not just *your* first weeks, of course, everyone's first few weeks in this job are crucially important. We all know that if you fluff your entrance, recovery can be really difficult. So, we should all invest big time in making sure that new fundraisers hit the ground running and get off to the very best possible start. Every new entrant should be able to say, 'Making the most of my first three or four weeks in fundraising got me really fired up, helped me sort out what really matters, pointed me towards what I should be doing and where I should go next.' Put another way, it's as important to inspire your new fundraisers as it is to inspire your new donors.

ORIGINS AND OBJECTIVES

Over the years since SOFII started we've repeatedly heard senior fundraisers say how useful the site is for newbies. It would be churlish to suggest that some simply log onto SOFII then plonk their new recruits in front of a computer screen for their first few weeks, though versions of that do certainly happen. So, we might as well ensure their time is well spent.

SIGNIFICANCE AND SPECIAL CHARACTERISTICS

Far too many talented young entrants don't stay long in fundraising. Everyone would benefit if we could reduce this too high tally of false or faltering career starts.

> **'If you trust in yourself...and believe in your dreams... and follow your star...you'll still get beaten by people who spent their time working hard, learning things and weren't so lazy.'**
>
> Terry Pratchett, author

BACKGROUND STORY

A fundraiser's first few weeks are likely to be stressful, both for employer and employee. To fill up the daily work schedule for the new recruit, the boss has to put his or her own 'to do' list on hold to take care of an as yet unproductive member of staff. Inevitably more a hindrance than a help during these first few weeks, the new recruit is apt to be at best bewildered, if not completely at sea for most of the time. So, to ensure those first

weeks are not to be a failure for all concerned, the fresher's time needs to be carefully and creatively organised. Getting this right will have massive benefits for our profession.

IMPACT, INFLUENCE AND OPPORTUNITIES

If employers can make the first vital weeks work superbly well it will inevitably have massive impact and influence on how charities attract, retain and develop their most talented and best motivated recruits. Fundraising leaders should commit to giving all new recruits a stunning first few weeks to remember. This calls for careful planning and deep understanding. Or you could just give all your new recruits a copy of this book!

LINK TO MORE ON A GOOD START FOR FUNDRAISERS

https://sofii.org/the-fundraisers-toolbox/my-first-weeks-as-a-fundraiser

HOW THE AGITATOR SEES IT:

http://agitator.thedonorvoice.com/why-i-love-winnie-the-pooh

PART 4

Case studies of creativity, innovation and inspiration

The exhibits that follow feature tangible ideas and campaigns rather than concepts, principles and basic fundamentals. The generous, open sharing of detailed case studies of successes and failures is a proud phenomenon of the for-change sector worldwide. Issues of competitive advantage seem unimportant in this unusual business area. Maintaining an edge by preserving sector secrets is rarely a priority, seldom even considered. Newcomers requesting help and information are met, usually, by willing offers of positive support from seemingly competing organisations. Success stories are shared freely and openly in the interests of encouraging copying and adapting. This unselfish sharing is one of the for-change sector's greatest achievements and also one of its most precious assets. It should be preserved, publicised and extended.

The case histories selected for this section are just droplets from a truly vast reservoir. Among the nearly 1,000 detailed case histories of successful and sometimes unsuccessful campaigning fundraising collected on SOFII the serious searcher for world-changing ideas will find their finest inspiration. A cornucopia of still fresh initiatives you'll wish you'd thought of, these carefully documented campaigns, ideas and innovations are all freely shared so that they might be borrowed, embellished and reused. A selection of them have been labelled as 'the best of the best', exemplary success stories from sector stars from all around the world. A few of these and some others are shared here so that campaigning fundraisers can fly a little bit higher by standing upon the shoulders of eagles.

24 Giving donors choices: the Botton Village story

WHY I CHOSE THIS

Back in 2009, in prophetic mode, I wrote, 'donors have gained and will gain increasing control of our means of communicating with them'. This story illustrates an early, splendidly effective prototype for that, dating back to the mid-1980s. Plus – and this is no coincidence – it's the best case history of fundraising success that I know of. The Botton Village experiment allowed donors control over what they receive from their charity and when, so it's the earliest known example of a functional fundraising preference scheme. As it worked so well it should be the last word in the tedious, ongoing 'opt-in or opt-out' saga, but as with so many important developments, many in charities – if they know of it at all – are simply ignorant of its significance.

ORIGINS AND OBJECTIVES

Botton Village, part of the Camphill Family, is a working rural community of adults with a mental disability, where villagers and co-workers live and work together in harmony with their environment. They started fundraising comparatively recently, in the early 1980s, and then only because they had to, as their statutory support was being taken away. The Botton villagers and co-workers approached the prospect of fundraising with awe and gratitude for anyone who might want to support their work financially. They made an early and firm commitment to doing 'the right thing' by their donors. They even asked, 'what can we do in return, for them?' This was to prove a transformational paradigm shift.

SIGNIFICANCE AND SPECIAL CHARACTERISTICS

Botton Village is the true home of relationship fundraising. Its story was a significant inspiration for the book of that name that I published in 1992. At the core of Botton's commitment to their donors was the belief that, as giving is entirely voluntary, wherever possible donors should be given the choice on any aspect of their relationship with the charity that they could possibly have influence or control over.

BACKGROUND STORY

Until this time donors everywhere were invariably not given any say in how they might be communicated with. The fundraisers decided that, not the

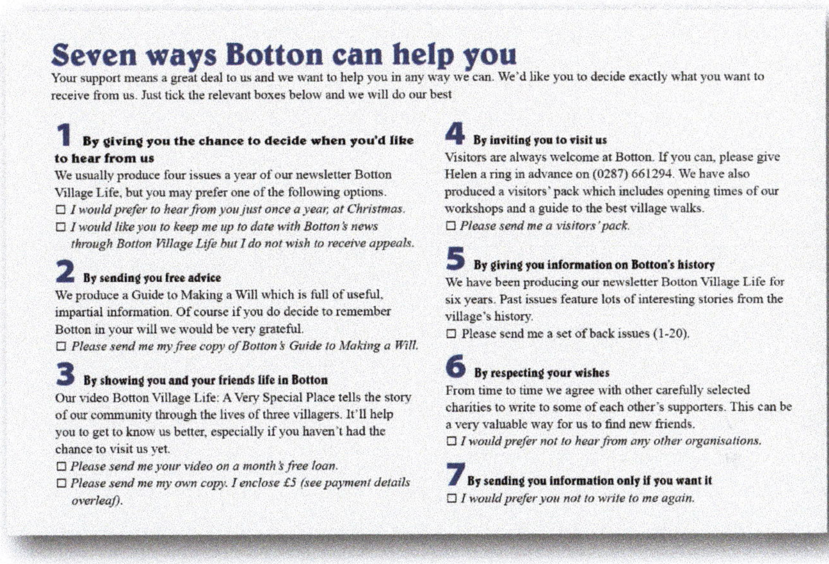

Seven ways Botton can help you

Your support means a great deal to us and we want to help you in any way we can. We'd like you to decide exactly what you want to receive from us. Just tick the relevant boxes below and we will do our best

1 By giving you the chance to decide when you'd like to hear from us
We usually produce four issues a year of our newsletter Botton Village Life, but you may prefer one of the following options.
☐ *I would prefer to hear from you just once a year, at Christmas.*
☐ *I would like you to keep me up to date with Botton's news through Botton Village Life but I do not wish to receive appeals.*

2 By sending you free advice
We produce a Guide to Making a Will which is full of useful, impartial information. Of course if you do decide to remember Botton in your will we would be very grateful.
☐ *Please send me my free copy of Botton's Guide to Making a Will.*

3 By showing you and your friends life in Botton
Our video Botton Village Life: A Very Special Place tells the story of our community through the lives of three villagers. It'll help you to get to know us better, especially if you haven't had the chance to visit us yet.
☐ *Please send me your video on a month's free loan.*
☐ *Please send me my own copy. I enclose £5 (see payment details overleaf).*

4 By inviting you to visit us
Visitors are always welcome at Botton. If you can, please give Helen a ring in advance on (0287) 661294. We have also produced a visitors' pack which includes opening times of our workshops and a guide to the best village walks.
☐ *Please send me a visitors' pack.*

5 By giving you information on Botton's history
We have been producing our newsletter Botton Village Life for six years. Past issues feature lots of interesting stories from the village's history.
☐ Please send me a set of back issues (1-20).

6 By respecting your wishes
From time to time we agree with other carefully selected charities to write to some of each other's supporters. This can be a very valuable way for us to find new friends.
☐ *I would prefer not to hear from any other organisations.*

7 By sending you information only if you want it
☐ *I would prefer you not to write to me again.*

donors. Botton Village started offering its donors choices using the simple form shown above. That this reply form went against the prevailing ethos of the time is evident from the headline. Tradition would have dictated it should say, *'Seven ways that you can help Botton Village'*. It says the exact opposite. Just how subversive this was at the time was evidenced by a debate held at the Institute of Fundraising's National Convention. This form's appearance was met with howls of disbelief and disapproval from the assembled throng of fundraisers, outraged by the idea of offering donors a chance to opt out of receiving appeals. Perceived as heresy, what some in that audience failed to appreciate was that Botton had analysed their donors' giving patterns (humble Botton Village was even then way ahead of the field in their management of data, thanks to their assiduous and dedicated fundraiser, Lawrence Stroud) and had found that many of their donors only gave once annually, usually pre-Christmas, despite receiving at least five appeals through the year. This, they concluded, was a quite deliberate choice by their donors. 'So why not let the donors tell us what they'd choose?', Lawrence and his co-workers reasoned. 'Let's give them choices, so rather than following our preconceptions, they can tell us what they really want.' It wasn't such a big risk – for in offering the 'Christmas only' route, Botton knew that the last quarter of the year is nearly as big as the other three put together. It's a universal phenomenon: 50 per cent of non-profits get the majority of their annual donations in the last three months of the year and 30 per cent of annual giving happens in December.[1]

1 According to research from US fundraising supplier Winspire.

Crucially, inspirationally, Botton had never tested this, for the simple reason that Botton believed giving donors choices was the right thing to do; whether or not it might increase or reduce giving was incidental. Giving increased hugely.

IMPACT, INFLUENCE AND OPPORTUNITIES

Thus was born a fundraising classic that should have changed the practices of a whole business sector. It led to fundraising response rates, gift levels, legacy pledges and donor retention rates so far ahead of industry norms as to be genuinely outstanding. Botton Village remains one of only two organisations that I've worked with that have been so successful they've had to stop fundraising because their needs have been more than met. Yet only a fraction of fundraising organisations have implemented any of the treasure trove of lessons from the Botton Village story. Our sector shares information widely and deeply, but that doesn't necessarily mean that fundraisers learn from it.

Offering donors choices is costly and challenging, so calls for commitment and persistence. Most fundraisers lack the capacity and the strength of character to implement such a programme consistently. Yet in the wake of 2015's media assaults on bad fundraising practices it became even more clear that Botton Village has for decades been pointing the way that all fundraisers should follow. Such change, sadly, doesn't happen quickly. But at last, happening it is. Despite limited uptake of the Fundraising Regulator's proposed preference scheme, the public's desire for choice over how they're communicated with won't ever go away. What Botton Village showed is that it's possible to profit hugely from this inherent donor aspiration because, when it's done sincerely and well, donors love being given practical choices that grant them control of what they receive.

LINKS TO MORE ON GIVING DONORS CHOICES

https://sofii.org/case-study/botton-village-giving-donors-choices
https://sofii.org/cde/project-13-giving-choices-and-managing-preference
https://www.youtube.com/watch?v=LHPgCSIfhIc

HOW THE AGITATOR SEES IT:

http://agitator.thedonorvoice.com/what-to-listen-for-in-donor-onboarding

25 Showing donors the difference they make: Feed the Children's 'baby box'

WHY I CHOSE THIS

This is a story of classic product development – the creation of a powerful giving proposition – in this case, one that delivers life-saving essentials while showing donors the difference they make. The basic idea came from the best possible place – charity workers on the front line. A very creative copywriter then added some sensible innovations and turned it into a compact fundraising classic. By providing practical, tangible and easily imaginable necessities the case for support behind this proposition proved irresistible, delivering lasting public appeal.

ORIGINS AND OBJECTIVES

In then war-torn Bosnia the baby box was devised specifically to respond to the need to maintain giving at a time when donor interest was flagging as the remorseless civil war dragged on. The opportunity was the emerging need to provide nursing mothers with basic essentials that could not be obtained locally. The campaign was created by Feed the Children's

advertising agency, Burnett Associates Group. The writer was Karin Weatherup.

BACKGROUND STORY

The initiative was devised towards the end of the five-year civil war that tore former Yugoslavia apart. After months of enterprising, very successful donor recruitment and development by Feed the Children UK (later renamed as Children's Aid Direct), response to their traditional appeals began, perhaps not surprisingly, to fall off as donors became increasingly used to seeing images from the war zone on their nightly television broadcasts. Feed the Children's agency realised that to improve results they had to do something dramatic to revive interest in their client and its work. So, they set about creating a new fundraising product, built around a classic 'shopping list' approach that embodied the timeless, unfailing mantra of the direct marketing fundraiser: show donors why their gift is needed now, what it'll cost and what it will achieve.

SIGNIFICANCE AND SPECIAL CHARACTERISTICS

Though far from the first example of a product-led fundraising proposition (best-known being child sponsorship, though there are many others, mostly geared towards monthly giving, see exhibit 19), this campaign introduced several fresh components. It has immediate, powerful donor appeal because it clearly answers the questions donors most commonly ask: 'Where does my money go and what does it achieve?' In addition to the listed enclosures (see ad on previous page) as an additional involvement device donors could also include a special message. A significant proportion did, adding photographs, postcards and often touching personal messages. Many Bosnian mothers replied to these, via the charity. These moving, often dramatic exchanges of goodwill messages from the front line were frequently featured in the national and local press, which brought in many new donors for Feed the Children at no extra cost.

IMPACT, INFLUENCE AND OPPORTUNITIES

The baby boxes were real. Each box bought by a donor meant that a real box stuffed with necessities could be delivered to a parent in Bosnia with multiple urgent needs. This promotion prompted a surge in interest in creating appropriate products that really resonate with donors. Few have been as successful as the baby box.

PRODUCTS, PRICING AND PROPOSITIONS

Donors want to see what their money will buy, what it will achieve and to be reminded that their gifts deliver real value for money. Promising this is not only reasonable and just, it makes excellent fundraising sense. So, it pays fundraisers to develop a shopping-list that donors can chose from, that sets out tangible, realistic, relevant yet urgent needs carefully and sensibly priced, which can be offered to donors at any appropriate time. If your proposition is a regular giving scheme it's sensible to construct an annual communications programme alongside it, through which you will keep your regular donors engaged, informed and inspired – so keeping them actively involved as 'friends for life'.

See further examples of effective fundraising propositions via the following links

https://sofii.org/case-study/actionaids-welcome-to-child-sponsorship-package

https://sofii.org/case-study/actionaid-bollocks-to-poverty-campaign

https://sofii.org/case-study/greenpeace-frontline-launch-of-a-high-level-monthly-giving-scheme

https://sofii.org/article/what-can-fundraisers-learn-from-product-marketing

Such innovations however are not easy to create. They require investment, creativity and testing, but when it works well such a scheme can really transform the donor experience and the fortunes of the organisation that has developed it. Of course, sometimes events beyond the fundraiser's control can curtail the fundraising potential, just as they can sometimes enhance it. When the war ended, offering the baby boxes made less sense, very suddenly. Which of course is as it should be.

LINK TO MORE ON THIS CASE STUDY

https://sofii.org/case-study/feed-the-childrens-baby-box

HOW THE AGITATOR SEES IT:

http://agitator.thedonorvoice.com/get-donors-to-care-about-their-impact-not-your-overhead

26 Storytelling that shook a nation: long copy press ads from Amnesty and the Bhopal Medical Appeal

WHY I CHOSE THIS

In the late 1980s I joined Amnesty International solely because I'd been shaken, outraged and inspired by one of these seminal ads. Many years later I had the privilege of working closely with the team that created them. Then, working with a new generation of Amnesty communicators, we set about crafting new ads based on the style and success of these earlier iconic communications and, decades later, showed they could still work. The distinctive, gut-wrenching, irresistible stories that form the spine of these powerful, discomforting advertisements are a copywriter's dream. In the late 1980s and early 90s Amnesty recruited scores of new donors like me, cost-effectively off the page, a huge achievement, even then. A few years later, the same writer – a top agency creative with no special training in fundraising – created a series of whole page long-copy advertisements that launched and successfully funded the Bhopal Medical Appeal on the 10th anniversary of the worst man-made disaster in history, when clouds of poison gas escaping from the Union Carbide factory devastated the Indian city of Bhopal. Though very different organisations and causes, without the Amnesty ads the Bhopal Medical Appeal would never have got started.

ORIGINS AND OBJECTIVES

For any organisation to commission a creative team such as this and to give them the space, time and freedom they need to create such game-changing press advertisements calls for foresight, courage and enterprise. The genesis and genius of these ads lies in the relentless assembling of layers of emotion that copywriter Indra Sinha builds into his stories, to the point when, as he says, 'the reader's anger simply boils off the page'. Indra's great skill is how he turns that anger into action. Working with Indra and designer Neil Godfrey while they go through the process of researching, testing, probing, refining, rejecting, redrafting, complaining, scrapping it all and starting all over again until it's precisely right is testing for any client and very few pass with credit. As Amnesty and the Bhopal Medical Appeal can show, the results when they do are beyond gratifying, the stuff of legend. It takes exceptional leadership within the charities to foster the necessary humility, patience and acceptance of risk that charity clients have

to cultivate if they wish to construct the environment within which such creativity can flourish.

SIGNIFICANCE AND SPECIAL CHARACTERISTICS

Charities are traditionally risk-averse, cautious, timid, conservative and unadventurous. Which of course makes no sense, since their job is to change the world, urgently. Sometimes, under the right leadership, the climate in an NGO can be just right to do things differently. For both Amnesty and the BMA, these ads came at such a time. Our sector's notorious risk aversion perhaps derives from the supposedly inevitable tightness of budgets, or the caution that inherently flows from its uniquely accountable governance structure, or even the simple small 'c' conservatism that seems to come from always trying to do the right thing. The overwhelming counterbalance to these inhibiting caveats should be the drama and urgency of our causes and the injustice of tolerating their casual continued acceptance. In this business, there should be no excuse for playing safe.

BACKGROUND STORY

When these ads were first commissioned Amnesty was already long-established, well known and admired for its work around the world on human rights abuses and injustices. By contrast the Bhopal Medical Appeal started with nothing beyond an initial long copy ad created by Indra Sinha, who persuaded the ad agency that then employed him to underwrite the ad's cost in return for an IOU. The advertisement succeeded, the IOU wasn't needed and the BMA was born. Over 25 years a series of similar-style ads generated sufficient funds to build two free clinics serving the still desperate and struggling people of Bhopal. 'We took risks,' said Sinha, 'because risks created opportunities. You have to know what you are writing about from the inside...to tell as much truth as pain will permit, you have to know, love and trust your readers, because you are placing other people's lives in their hands.'

Through the 1990s and early 2000s Indra Sinha became renowned for hard-hitting, campaigning advertising for major causes. In 2007 his novel *Animal's People* was shortlisted for the Booker Prize, an achievement he links directly to the Amnesty ads experience. In July 2015, Indra was awarded an honorary Doctorate in Literature by the University of Brighton for 'his major contribution to literature and demonstrating the power of words in changing people's lives'.

> **'The written word is the deepest dagger you can drive into a person's soul. All charity advertising has ultimately only one task: to force people to make a decision about whether or not they will take responsibility for the way things are. The difficulty is that people know this and armour themselves against it. Piercing their carapace will take every ounce of your courage, ingenuity and strength.'**
>
> Indra Sinha on the writing process, quoted in Ken Burnett's *Storytelling can change the world*

IMPACT, INFLUENCE AND OPPORTUNITIES

These ads launched a thousand copywriting careers. Arguably, Indra Sinha is the greatest fundraising copywriter still writing today. 'These methods,' he says, 'get results, but they're not what fundraisers are usually taught.' He has a very good point. They should be.

> **'Your ads do not have to reflect the prevailing culture. You can attack it. Subvert it. Set out to change it. This isn't your job, but you**

can make it your job. It is far more important than the job you are supposed to be doing…the copywriter has real power.'

Indra Sinha advising young writers, from his essay, *The Last Word*

However brilliant the writer and designer, inevitably great creativity is unlikely to flourish without a great client. Oh, for more fundraising clients capable of issuing a brief like this!

A few years after these ads appeared leading fundraising copywriter

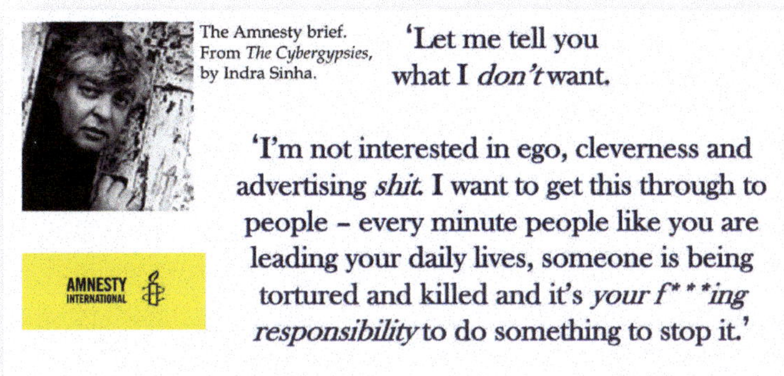

Karin Weatherup created Amnesty's now famous multi-award-winning pen pack, heavily influenced by the storytelling style of Indra Sinha. The pen pack became Amnesty's banker recruitment pack used by different branches of Amnesty around the world for more than a decade. Whatever revenue stream you focus on, it pays to study the greats.

LINKS TO MORE ON THESE CLASSIC STORYTELLING ADS

https://sofii.org/article/how-i-wrote-it-the-classic-amnesty-press-ads
https://sofii.org/case-study/amnesty-international-uk-press-ads-that-shook-a-nation
https://sofii.org/article/the-last-word-how-copywriters-can-change-the-world
https://sofii.org/case-study/amnesty-international-the-pen-pack
https://sofii.org/case-study/bhopal-medical-appeal-press-advertisements

27 Transformational campaigns: NSPCC, GOSH and the courage to think and aim *really big*

WHY I CHOSE THIS

Every campaigning fundraiser should dream of the big appeal, the game-changer, the massive step change that will enable a real leap forward in what your cause is able to do, who it can reach and its impact on the issue it addresses. If your organisation's dream is to cure cancer or end child abuse, don't imagine you can't aim that high. There are no prizes for aiming low and doing what's expected. Ending slavery, equal rights, LGBT rights, Make Poverty History, Votes for Women, Extinction Rebellion, Black Lives Matter, #MeToo: all must have seemed impossible dreams at the outset, all have produced massive progress through campaigns that wouldn't accept anything less than total victory. There's lots still to do – reversing climate change, eradicating malaria, ending hunger, patrimony, racism, inequality, wars, injustice... All such issues might be within campaigning reach and will be achieved one day. For sure, even seemingly impossible dreams can inspire and bind donors, so will be worth pursuing.

ORIGINS AND OBJECTIVES

Organisational transformation is the process of dramatically changing an existing corporate culture to achieve a competitive advantage or address a significant challenge. It will invariably be a high-energy, high-adrenalin time for any organisation and its people, especially when the change means more lives can be saved or more of a difference can be made.

SIGNIFICANCE AND SPECIAL CHARACTERISTICS

Superlatives such as 'ground-breaking', 'game-changing' and 'transformational' are often sprayed around in marketing and communications circles, so much so they can lose their power and meaning. The NSPCC's Full Stop campaign – designed to end child abuse

– is an exception. Here, those words really do apply and more. A rising tide lifts all boats. Once an organisation's ambition has been dramatically stretched it's unlikely that it will settle back. For everyone who works on such a campaign, at all levels, the difference can be truly life-changing.

BACKGROUND STORY

NSPCC's Full Stop campaign is the story of old-fashioned, volunteer – not staff-driven – fundraising. Giles Pegram CBE, former director of appeals at the NSPCC, has launched transformational public appeals not once but twice, for the same organisation. His remarkable story in launching the

NSPCC™

Cruelty to children must stop. FULL STOP.

The NSPCC Full Stop campaign. A fundraising and campaigning triumph, in six parts.

two biggest ever charitable appeals in Britain is linked below. Campaigns like these aren't about incremental change or gradual growth. They don't involve chance, or quick fixes, or one-hit-wonders. This is about ample lead time and careful, sustained investment, about planned, persistent transformation, a doubling, trebling or quadrupling of activity and income in one carefully structured, strategised and constructed campaign with appropriate commitment, inspired and visionary leadership, sustained and bold acceptance of risk.

IMPACT, INFLUENCE AND OPPORTUNITIES

The NSPCC's campaigns have inspired other organisations to dramatically up their game, not least Great Ormond Street Hospital's Wishing Well appeal, which you can read about by following the link below. Transformational campaigns are far from easy to pull off, neither are they for the faint hearted. Over and above the sustained investment they take guts, vision, long-view planning, brave risk-taking and dedication, which perhaps explains why they're so rare, particularly these days.

LINKS TO MORE ON TRANSFORMATIONAL CAMPAIGNS

https://sofii.org/case-study/the-nspcc-centenary-appeal-setting-the-gold-standard-in-major-campaign-fundraising-from-1984

https://sofii.org/case-study/nspccs-full-stop-campaign-sofiis-view (includes links to the six-part feature on NSPCC's Full Stop campaign)

https://sofii.org/case-study/the-wishing-well-appeal-for-great-ormond-street-childrens-hospital

28 The hero figure: RNLI and the 'He'll face...' inserts

WHY I CHOSE THIS

There's a huge, unique role for the hero figure in fundraising. Think Florence Nightingale, Marie Curie and the cancer-care nurses, Greenpeace and the wet-suited *warriors of the rainbow*, Médecins sans Frontières and the International Red Cross flying doctors into conflict zones, the heroic frontline aid workers, the White Helmets, or Captain Tom Moore... the list goes on. Hail the fundraising hero. Donors just love them.

ORIGINS AND OBJECTIVES

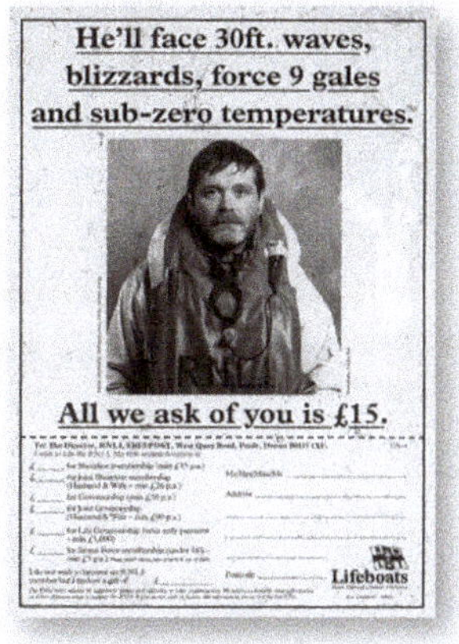

Donors seek out a hero figure and will believe in and donate to support her or him, happily. For decades the Royal National Lifeboat Institution (RNLI) believed itself to be so widely supported (just about every charity supporter in the UK respects and supports the Lifeboats) because of its mission to save lives at sea. Yet some years ago RNLI did its first ever research among supporters and found, surprise surprise, this isn't so. No, their researches told them, worthwhile though it undoubtedly is, your supporters care little for those who are rescued, rather they give their support because they're inspired by the hero rescuers – the brave and selfless men and women who volunteer to go out in all weathers, in stormy seas to rescue people in trouble they don't even know.

SIGNIFICANCE AND SPECIAL CHARACTERISTICS

This is more than just an example of a great donor recruitment proposition, it's also an exercise in understanding your WHY? (see exhibit 15) and a great encouragement to asking donors (ie doing some carefully-structured research – still an area of false economy and under-investment, for charities).

BACKGROUND STORY

The image of the lifeboatman is crucial to RNLI's fundraising success. Though there are lifeboatwomen, it has to be a man and he has to be bearded. He has to be framed by the image of a stormy sky and he has to be dripping wet, as if just swept in by a force nine gale. Plus, he has to look startled, as if he's only just made it. How do they know all this? Because response has been tested and the data scrupulously recorded. Follow the link below for the full story.

> **'We changed our attitudes, particularly our attitude to donors… content is essential when it comes to building and engaging relationships with donors. If you get your content right, your donors get a lot of benefits from your charity too.'**
>
> Jayne George, director of fundraising, marketing and media, RNLI

Recent RNLI campaigns have told donors 'the thing that keeps us going is your support'. Under the simple slogan, TO SAVE EVERY ONE, RNLI firmly places the emphasis on the volunteer lifeboatmen and women, taking the donor on board by saying explicitly, 'You are part of the crew'.

IMPACT, INFLUENCE AND OPPORTUNITIES

The RNLI example is perhaps the best-known and clearest instance of the effective use of a hero figure in campaigning fundraising. The hero acts in the donor's name. She or he delivers the aid, so embodies what the donor wants to do and can do from the comfort of an armchair, without personal risk. The power of the hero is well worth studying and emulating too. The heroic storyteller for both Amnesty and the Bhopal Medical Appeal (see exhibit 26) was the writer, the narrator or even an individual character that the writer had woven into his stories. If the storyteller gets it right, the organisation itself can be the hero. Dr Thomas Barnardo's homes for wayward waifs and strays really took off in the mid-1800s when the good doctor told his supporters the tragic story of 11-year-old John Somers, known as Carrots, who Barnardo had to turn away because his newly opened home was full to overflowing. Later that bitter night Carrots died hungry, cold and alone, his tiny corpse found next day, frozen stiff. The story led to Barnardo's policy of 'the ever-open door', a massively successful rallying cry for support. For donors, the real hero of this story was Dr B himself.

LINKS TO MORE ON THE POWER OF THE HERO FIGURE

https://sofii.org/case-study/the-rnli-hell-face-all-we-ask-of-you-press-insert

https://sofii.org/case-study/dr-barnardos-homes-how-the-death-of-carrots-led-to-a-powerful-slogan-from-1866

29 The irresistible proposition: Help the Aged's 'You have this gift/ Make a blind man see'

WHY I CHOSE THIS

Every now and then a fundraising organisation comes up with a truly spectacular offer to make to its supporters, then devises the most brilliant way of presenting it, simply but effectively, showing that fundraising is about the offer, not the ask. Help the Aged's '*Make a blind man see*' ad is a perfect example.

ORIGINS AND OBJECTIVES

In the 1970s Harold Sumption created the newspaper advertisement featured in this breakthrough campaign. The direct mail packs came later, building brilliantly on the original proposition and adding intrigue and involvement to take the cause right to the heart of the donor.

SIGNIFICANCE AND SPECIAL CHARACTERISTICS

Not for nothing were these two classic campaigns among the first to be featured in SOFII's *Best of the Best* category, which celebrates all-time brilliant fundraising and campaigning successes. This is the traditional fundraising direct offer with a reasonable price in the headline (must be at least four times that now). It looks simple, low cost, even amateur. Which of course requires real professionalism.

BACKGROUND STORY

Where on this earth could a serious concerned donor find such value for money? Just after this ad first appeared Harold told me that he'd wanted to create an urgent, irresistible, emotional offer that looked like it had been pulled together by two elderly ladies working on a rickety table in a leaky garret, an image suffused with care, economy and value for money. Tests showed that 20 centimetres x two columns was the hardest working

size, with the upmarket daily press as the prime media. Sometime later the direct mail packs above appeared, offering the same proposition with similar value for donations, accompanied by a small rectangle of opaque plastic enclosed with the immortal line, 'Inside there's a square of plastic that will open your eyes.'

IMPACT, INFLUENCE AND OPPORTUNITIES

Generations of fundraising creative writers have delighted at and celebrated these campaigns for their concise, unfussy, direct style and their simple, instantly effective appeal. These are instructive models for anyone wishing to craft a powerful, irresistible offer.

LINKS TO MORE ON IRRESISTIBLE PROPOSITIONS

https://sofii.org/case-study/help-the-aged-make-a-blind-man-see-press-advertisement

https://sofii.org/case-study/help-the-aged-you-have-this-gift-direct-mail-pack

30 The recycled fundraiser: Ryton Gardens' seed pots and BookAid's Reverse Book Club

WHY I CHOSE THESE

One huge, surely growing worry for fundraisers is the excess waste that our sector produces, with all the printing, paper, plastics and pollution that make up all the unread messages that campaigning fundraisers are responsible for, when they send out their appeals. The two campaigns featured here speak against waste in different ways and both achieved singular success.

ORIGINS AND OBJECTIVES

Any appeal for funds has to appeal to its recipients. Donors are savvy and discerning, so fundraisers have to do much better than merely perpetuate 'junk' marketing. Getting the right messages into the right hands in the right way is a key component of the campaigning fundraiser's skills. The scattergun concept isn't good enough. Wasted messages are costly pollution, so must be avoided or at least minimised. Lookalike messages inevitably become tired and wasteful. In fundraising the beginning of success is to be different. The beginning of failure is to be the same.

SIGNIFICANCE AND SPECIAL CHARACTERISTICS

Campaigning fundraisers can combat waste by increased creativity, improving their messaging, targeting and data-handling to ensure their communications are appropriate and welcomed. We can avoid plastic. We can print always on recycled paper. We can listen better – donors frequently complain that fundraisers send way too much stuff. We can send less, but better. We can also make our promotions paragons of recyclable economy.

And, luckily for us, the campaigning fundraiser also has more than her share of opportunities for creativity and inspiration.

BACKGROUND STORY

Both of these campaigns demonstrate creativity based on a deep understanding of their donors. The Ryton Gardens exhibit has its genesis in its organisers' deep reluctance to embrace public fundraising, particularly by direct mail. BookAid's Reverse Book Club, copied directly from an earlier initiative in the USA, came into being because of a drastic cut in government funding. Both show that necessity is the mother of invention, that out of adversity can come advantage.

IMPACT, INFLUENCE AND OPPORTUNITIES

Both these campaigns have been inspiring fundraisers for at least a decade. The Ryton Gardens pack won many international awards and hit ten times its target. BookAid's Reverse Book Club concept was unashamedly stolen – or rather borrowed – from an American Bible Society idea from 20 years earlier and is the campaign that inspired the creation of SOFII.org. The Reverse Book Club idea is based on the traditional postal book club, but with the twist that rather than books going each month to the purchaser, they're sent instead to feed hungry minds in developing countries. Well, why should God have all the best ideas? Both campaigns have played their part in shaping the future of fundraising and they're still available to be copied or adapted by any aspiring newcomer who wants to make her or his mark. Indeed, follow the link below to find how BookAid went on to borrow and adapt another money-spinning idea, creating the Reverse Book Token. Good ideas don't have limits.

LINKS TO MORE ON THESE CAMPAIGNS

https://sofii.org/case-study/ryton-gardens-recyclable-mailing
https://sofii.org/article/why-should-god-have-all-the-best-ideas
https://sofii.org/case-study/book-aid-international-the-reverse-book-club

31 Reinventing face-to-face (F2F): Greenpeace develops a fundraising game-changer

WHY I CHOSE THIS

Face-to-face fundraising is as old as the hills. What could be more natural than one person talking to another – a potential donor, say, chatting with a fundraiser – engaging person-to-person, eyeball-to-eyeball, discussing an issue they both care about where the fundraiser earns the potential donor's freely-given consent to explain, within a reasonable time, the issue and its implications, the solutions her or his organisation proposes and the opportunities they provide for the donor to get involved and make a difference?

What could possibly be wrong with that? Most fundraisers won't appreciate that mass face-to-face fundraising was deployed successfully in the 1890s and onwards by the YMCA, developed by Charles Sumner Ward and colleagues. Because of its huge and recent impact many will be aware that, just over 25 years ago, this simple, essentially human interaction was refined and repurposed to great advantage by one major international non-profit. They promptly shared the secret of their success with other charities, until soon a new breed – the face-to-face fundraiser – became a familiar figure on the streets and doorsteps of most developed nations across the planet. But just as F2F all but replaced other already established methods of large-volume donor recruitment, signs of public disquiet at this seemingly new fundraising method began to appear and gather momentum. A generally unsupportive media coined the less than flattering term 'chuggers' (short for charity muggers) to describe the (mostly young, usually charming and friendly) people recruited to the task and it soon became clear that a fundraising

golden goose was slowly being squeezed of life, just as it was laying so many solid gold eggs.

But the main culprits in this were not the media, nor the public, nor the F2F agencies and suppliers. The drastic false economy that signalled the premature decline and potential demise of F2F originated in the fundraising charities themselves, as they relentlessly focused on the direct debits they were harvesting and on driving down what they might pay for each new sign-up, rather than on ensuring a good experience for those folks being asked to become regular donors. This is a tragedy for our times, a tale so laden with lessons and redolent of so many of our sector's shortcomings it should be compulsory reading for all.

ORIGINS AND OBJECTIVES

Sometime in the mid-1990s the rules for bank transfer in Austria changed to allow regular payments to be collected by direct electronic funds transfer. At that time the Austrian office of the environmental campaigning organisation Greenpeace International was looking to recruit monthly donors in volume, but they had very little funds for advertising or paid promotion and no tradition in the country of monthly giving. So Greenpeace Austria devised a new paradigm for individual donor acquisition, stopping passers-by and signing them up to regular giving in the shopping malls of Vienna and surrounding streets and public spaces. They did this thoroughly and well, at the height of a wave of environmental concern. Soon people were queuing up in the street, eager to talk to the young Greenpeace activists and campaigning fundraisers.

BACKGROUND STORY

Fundraising charities depend on their supporters. Growing its individual supporter file is the tried and tested route to sustainable fundraising for any cause. Yet year on year the average cost of recruiting one new supporter seems to rise inexorably. Through the ages, faced with this recurring dilemma, fundraisers' creative entrepreneurial ingenuity has always led to innovations that have shown a way forward.

More than quarter of a century ago, in Austria, Greenpeace made one such spectacular innovation possible and, despite several mostly self-imposed shortcomings, the idea born then has survived, prospered and, arguably, has the potential to adapt and survive quite a bit longer, while enabling the recruitment of literally millions of generally youngish new donors around the world. In 2019 UNICEF, perhaps the world's largest recruiter of donors face-to-face, recruited more than half a million new supporters by this method.

From its start in 1995 the idea quickly spread and soon it was impossible to control. This was a triumph, though built within it was a very considerable danger. Greenpeace's success at inspiring and signing up new supporters and their openness and willingness to share the secrets of that success led to volume donor recruitment changing dramatically in just about every market in the developed world. Their innovative, cost-effective way of signing up large numbers of supporters to electronic funds transfer halted and even reduced, for a time at least, the then spiralling cost of donor acquisition. In five years, in 18 countries, Greenpeace alone (as innovator they deserved and got a good head start) recruited 1.4 million new donors contributing annually in excess of US$150 million to the Greenpeace International network.[1] Not bad for a new idea. But soon just about every charity had got in on the act and before long there were signs that this new volume recruitment method wasn't finding favour with the public. Attrition rates spiralled, cost-per-donor rocketed and prospective donors increasingly crossed the road to avoid street fundraisers. They made it plain that they liked F2F's sister system, doorstep fundraising, even less.

SIGNIFICANCE AND SPECIAL CHARACTERISTICS

As we've seen, key to fundraising success is cost-effectively building a robust, viable file of regular committed individual donors, so the advent of F2F changed everything. At the time media and mail costs were soaring and increased competition was reducing responses so the essential component of any commercial business – the ability to recruit new customers at acceptable cost – had for many if not most fundraising organisations become economically unviable, or close to it (another way of looking at this might be that the cost of acquiring a new donor – the delay until costs

1 *Relationship Fundraising* second edition, 2002.

are recovered and payback can begin – was increasingly likely to be seen as unacceptable to the donating public). The arrival of direct dialogue – as face-to-face fundraising as practised by Greenpeace was initially called – enabled cost-effective recruitment in volume to become viable, once more. For a while, at least.

The early successes of Greenpeace and others inspired the growth of a massive and, for some, quite lucrative service industry as suppliers to the growing face-to-face sector. Few charities had the experience, entrepreneurial ability, capacity or desire to manage F2F teams for themselves, so specialist agencies grew up to serve the sector in this seemingly booming business. For some it was the route to rapid riches, but for most it quickly became evident that this was a sector focusing on the lowest common denominator, driving down the unit cost of donor acquisition without due care for long-term sustainability. Fundraising managers, often inexperienced and poorly equipped for managing the agency–client relationship (see exhibit 50), found themselves effectively buying new donors in bulk and obliged to negotiate to obtain the best deal. Soon ask, ask and ask again became the prevailing F2F paradigm. To anyone observing how this concept was developing, it seemed that the brief was:

Save the Children was the first non-profit to resume face-to-face fundraising in the Netherlands.

- ✶ All fundraisers should look alike, as menacing as possible, clipboards poised.
- ✶ Approach someone with whom you have no prior relationship, someone busily on their way somewhere...
- ✶ ...then with a fatuous chat-up line, persist in trying to open a conversation.
- ✶ Give them very little that might interest or intrigue.
- ✶ Press them to sign up indefinitely.
- ✶ Don't give up, don't go away.
- ✶ Call them quickly after to ask for more.
- ✶ Repeat again, again and again.

Small wonder donors grew to dislike street fundraisers and would go out of their way to avoid them.

IMPACT, INFLUENCE AND OPPORTUNITIES

Fundraisers might think that, despite the growth of the internet, the technology explosion and the associated transformation of communication in the intervening decades, no new paradigm for large-scale donor recruitment has emerged since this Greenpeace initiative. In the heads down, risk-averse nature of our times, it might be assumed this is because, fundraising organisations have lacked the necessary

SOME EFFECTIVE CHANNELS FOR ATTRACTING AND RECRUITING NEW DONORS IN VOLUME

- ✶ Word of mouth. Member-get-member. Free, but inconsistent and generally low volume.
- ✶ 'Dwell-time' ads strategically placed in public places, tube and bus cards, on backs of train and airline seats, in changing rooms, even public toilets, wherever people stop, sit and spend time (see exhibit 35).
- ✶ Press advertising 'off-the-page', usually with a response coupon (see exhibits 26, 28 and 29). This was the staple medium in the UK for decades until rising costs and falling readerships made it generally unviable except in disaster emergencies.
- ✶ Inserts, often intricate origami with built in reply envelopes, inserted loose or bound in key media (see exhibit 41).
- ✶ Television ads and infomercials, usually one minute plus in low-cost daytime slots, with a telephone response and a strong call to action (see exhibit 37).

Both telephone fundraising and direct mail have generally been found not to work well for new donor recruitment in the UK, though both still work well in other markets, particularly the USA.

commitment to investing in developing and testing new products and propositions that might work on scale. Which in turn might cause many fundraising organisations to fail to keep in at least reasonable check the ever-spiralling cost of recruiting new supporters. Not so. Strong evidence is emerging that shows the adventurous, creative spirit that characterises great campaigning fundraising is alive and well, devising new digital, DRTV and even telephone-led approaches to new donor recruitment that are proving to be to be splendidly cost-effective, particularly those focused on inspirational storytelling. The 2020 pandemic in particular has been a catalyst for change. In the links below, international fundraising leader Daryl Upsall explains the evolution of these and UNICEF's Daniel McDonnell and David Cravinho describe how UNICEF has developed a new approach to bring F2F up to date, which has lowered their acquisition cost despite the obvious restrictions of talking to a stranger in the street or on the doorstep during an infectious disease pandemic. We await future developments with bated breath – the health of our business model depends on it.

LINKS TO MORE ON REINVENTING F2F

https://sofii.org/case-study/greenpeace-international-the-reinvention-of-face-to-face-fundraising

https://sofii.org/article/f2f-stuck-in-deep-snow-between-vinkovci-and-blod

https://sofii.org/case-study/senses-brilliant-style-for-face-to-face-fundraising

https://sofii.org/article/the-day-world-vision-welcomed-me-to-their-world

https://sofii.org/article/why-coronavirus-has-been-unicefs-catalyst-for-change

https://sofii.org/article/how-face-to-face-fundraising-got-the-moves-during-coronavirus

HOW THE AGITATOR SEES IT:

http://agitator.thedonorvoice.com/is-f-2-f-acquisition-a-sustainer-oasis-or-a-mirage

32 Donor-focused fundraising: meet Nana Murphy, your ideal supporter

WHY I CHOSE THIS

When I made my living as a direct mail copywriter I prospered at my craft largely because I imagined that every letter I wrote was a one-to-one communication between me and a donor I knew really well – my mother. Though she only gave small amounts each time my mum was a generous, responsive donor. I knew just what might appeal to her and just how to present it. Whether mailed to one or one million, each communication should in essence be considered as just one person writing to another they understand well, telling them about something they both care deeply about, the writer showing the reader what she or he can do to make a difference however much or however little they can give. Unlike my mum Nana Murphy is a composite, an imaginary friend, yet her character and persona have grown to gargantuan proportions, so much so that her impact on successful fundraising in Ireland and elsewhere has been profound. It pays fundraisers to identify and cherish a believable individual to write to, even if it's an imaginary friend.

ORIGINS AND OBJECTIVES

I don't know who it was who first mentioned Dorothy Donor from Tunbridge Wells, but she was another entirely fictitious construct who, though a stereotype and a cliché, inspired me and my generation of fundraisers. The final part of each chapter in *Relationship Fundraising* contains a pen-portrait of a donor, to make a variety of points I felt important at the time. Not one of them was real, but they all came alive in the imaginations of generations of campaigning fundraisers.

SIGNIFICANCE AND SPECIAL CHARACTERISTICS

Nana Murphy transformed fundraising at the Irish charity Merchants Quay Ireland. She is also perhaps the best documented imaginary donor of all time. So, she could transform your fundraising too.

BACKGROUND STORY

In 2008, during the worst fundraising environment Ireland had ever known, homelessness charity Merchants Quay Ireland turned for help to Denisa Casement, Lisa Sargent and Sandra Collette, three world-class experts all passionately committed to donor-focused fundraising. Having bravely committed themselves to putting Merchants Quay Ireland's donors first, the three then created the persona of Nana Murphy to bring the concept alive. Then they fell in love with her and simply couldn't do enough for her, nor could they do without her. Inspired and led by Nana Murphy, the results these four achieved are consistently spectacular, making this an essential guide to achieving brilliant fundraising in troubled times.

IMPACT, INFLUENCE AND OPPORTUNITIES

This is one of the best from a growing body of case histories of donor-focused fundraising. It's significant because it covers a number of practical initiatives over several years and shows the value of creating a very clear picture of your supporter with all her interests, passions and foibles and pitching all your communications, messages and writing specifically to her.

Characters such as Nana Murphy can really help you to put the supporter at the heart of your strategies and create an excellent, sustainable supporter experience.

LINK TO MORE ON DONOR-FOCUSED FUNDRAISING

https://sofii.org/case-study/lessons-from-merchants-quay-ireland

HOW THE AGITATOR SEES IT:

http://agitator.thedonorvoice.com/donor-centricity-the-missing-ingredient

33 Brave, jaw-dropping creativity: Nazis against Nazis

WHY I CHOSE THIS

Simply, because I love it! How would you turn an intimidating extremist neo-Nazi march into a promotional fundraising event that raises money to help people escape from extremist groups? Simple – get your supporters to sponsor the marchers themselves, so that for every step they take, €10.00 is raised to counter their extremism.

ORIGINS AND OBJECTIVES

Every year around 250 neo-Nazis strut their stuff in the streets of Wunsiedel, a small town in Bavaria, Germany. Disliking this event intensely the townspeople turned the tables on the marchers – not with violence, but with a brilliant campaigning and fundraising idea.

SIGNIFICANCE AND SPECIAL CHARACTERISTICS

For a town feeling helpless in the face of swaggering right-wing extremists, the solution turned out to be a fundraising event, not though for the funds it raised, but for the uniqueness of the event itself, which was cleverly constructed to get the fascists themselves to raise the funds that would put them out of business. With a record sum raised and extensive national publicity the humiliation of the marchers was very publicly assured.

Nazis against Nazis – Germany's most involuntary charity walk.

BACKGROUND STORY

Neo-Nazis from across Europe flock each year to Wunsiedel in a pilgrimage to celebrate Hitler's deputy Rudolf Hess, who was buried there. The townsfolk hated the notoriety this unwelcome influx brought, but felt powerless to prevent it. Then, without telling the marchers, the German non-profit Exit arranged for anti-Nazi supporters around the country to sponsor the marchers themselves, so that as they walked through the town, they were marching against themselves. As the march progressed the marchers slowly came to realise that all the banners and signs around them were actually directed against them rather than in support. As they neared the end it became clear that they'd been raising money against themselves. Fundraising seldom gets more satisfying than this.

IMPACT, INFLUENCE AND OPPORTUNITIES

At the festival of fundraising celebration that is *I Wish I'd Thought Of That* (IWITOT) it's often hard to choose the winner among all the great entries. Not in 2015 at the International Fundraising Congress's IWITOT in the Netherlands though – each audience member was given a vote and there was instantly no doubt which exhibit would be the winner. You guessed it – Nazis against Nazis!

The campaign not only raised ten times what they'd raised previously from events in the town, they also attracted huge publicity with leading magazines, newspapers and TV programmes in Germany reporting on the event. They won numerous fundraising awards too.

LINK TO MORE ON THIS CAMPAIGN

https://sofii.org/case-study/nazis-against-nazis-the-most-involuntary-walkathon

34 Different strokes for different folks: BHF's in memoriam, corporate involvement, virtual events and posters

WHY I CHOSE THIS

This isn't the most extensive nor the most impressive collection of campaigns from a single organisation, but a dive into the British Heart Foundation's array of exhibits on SOFII quickly shows the breadth, depth and diversity of fundraising communications challenges that face a major campaigning and fundraising charity.

ORIGINS AND OBJECTIVES

As if to show how flexible, inventive and creative campaigning fundraisers have to be, BHF's output in recent years illustrates their responses to a rich variety of challenges, all designed to entertain, inspire and engage a range of audiences in a complex cornucopia of opportunities. These four campaigns are only a fraction of them.

SIGNIFICANCE AND SPECIAL CHARACTERISTICS

An intriguing slide calculator that will knock the socks off busy businesspeople, posters that will engage health-conscious young foodies, education aids that fascinate and draw in sceptical schoolkids and their overworked teachers, appropriate ways to celebrate and remember the recently departed, plus Marathon event opportunities for the unathletic. Communicating a cause is undeniably varied and full of possibilities.

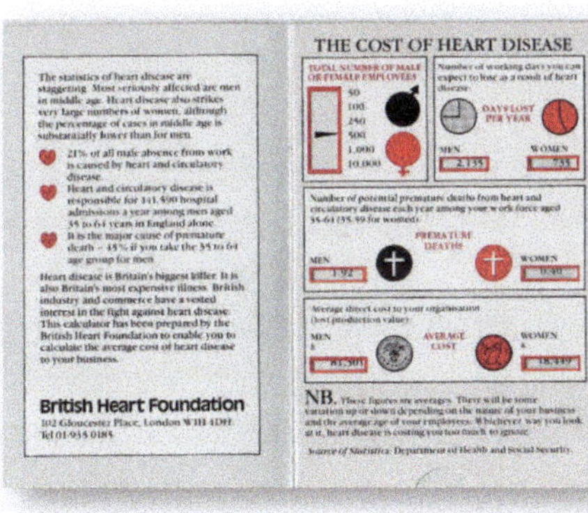

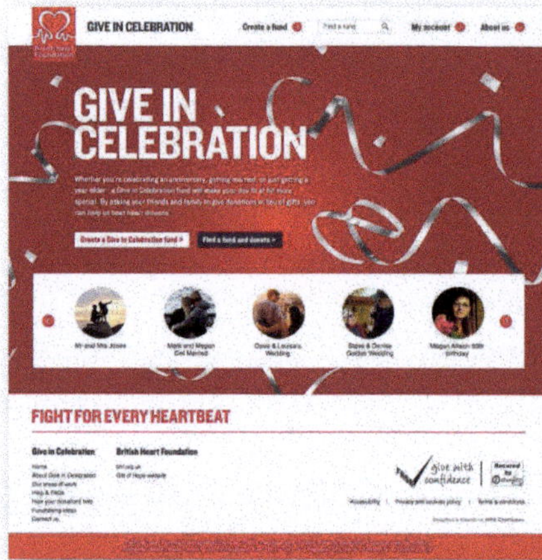

BACKGROUND STORY

As involvement devices go, the BHF calculator is a classic, an irresistibly intriguing example of how to personalise your and your company's role in the fight against heart disease. Long before the now ubiquitous virtual event, BHF's MyMarathon initiative allowed supporters to complete the distance at their own convenience – and they didn't even have to run! The BHF hamburger, from a series of posters that each packs a powerful lesson, is not only quirky, attractive, clever and hugely informative, it features what has to be the tastiest-looking and biggest burger of all time. Their 'Gift of Hope' in memoriam and celebrations promotion is a masterclass in strategy for an activity unique to fundraisers. The links below explain the individual stories and detail behind these successful promotions, while collectively they represent the wonderfully rich variety of communications that facilitate successful campaigning fundraising.

IMPACT, INFLUENCE AND OPPORTUNITIES

Hard to say precisely but certainly huge. All these promotions will have encouraged interactions from a range of people including captains of industry, employees, would-be athletes, fitness enthusiasts, couch potatoes, teachers, school children, givers in celebration and in memory plus a host of others. And campaigning fundraisers of all types and shades. The exhibits linked below lead to many more, all varied, informative and instructive.

LINKS TO MORE ON THESE CAMPAIGNS

https://sofii.org/case-study/british-heart-foundations-calculate-the-cost-of-heart-disease-mailing
https://sofii.org/case-study/british-heart-foundation-my-marathon
https://sofii.org/case-study/british-heart-foundation-the-poster-series
https://sofii.org/case-study/british-heart-foundation-gift-of-hope-give-in-celebration

35 Dwell time: David Ogilvy leaves a letter on a train

WHY I CHOSE THIS

Here's a tale of a master copywriter himself telling a moving story in an unusual place to frankly astonishing effect. David Ogilvy of course ranks high among the great fundraising writers (see also exhibit 47), but this campaign has many extra noteworthy attributes beyond the quality of his copy, not least the use of 'dwell time' long before the concept was defined.

ORIGINS AND OBJECTIVES

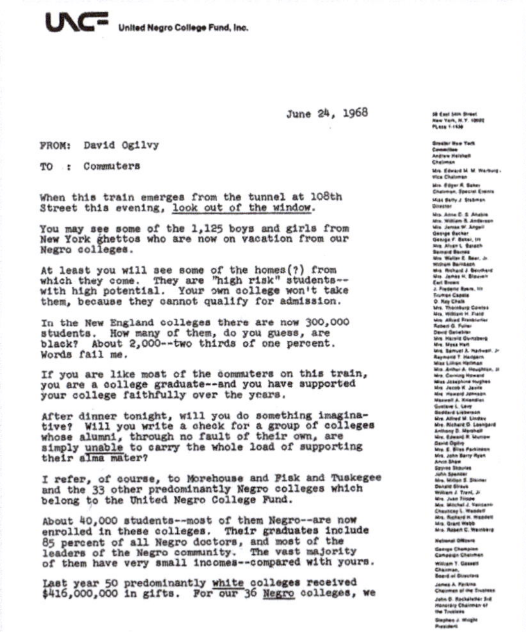
United Negro College Fund, Inc.

June 24, 1968

FROM: David Ogilvy

TO : Commuters

When this train emerges from the tunnel at 108th Street this evening, look out of the window.

You may see some of the 1,125 boys and girls from New York ghettos who are now on vacation from our Negro colleges.

At least you will see some of the homes(?) from which they come. They are "high risk" students--with high potential. Your own college won't take them, because they cannot qualify for admission.

In the New England colleges there are now 300,000 students. How many of them, do you guess, are black? About 2,000--two thirds of one percent. Words fail me.

If you are like most of the commuters on this train, you are a college graduate--and you have supported your college faithfully over the years.

After dinner tonight, will you do something imaginative? Will you write a check for a group of colleges whose alumni, through no fault of their own, are simply unable to carry the whole load of supporting their alma mater?

I refer, of course, to Morehouse and Fisk and Tuskegee and the 33 other predominantly Negro colleges which belong to the United Negro College Fund.

About 40,000 students--most of them Negro--are now enrolled in these colleges. Their graduates include 85 percent of all Negro doctors, and most of the leaders of the Negro community. The vast majority of them have very small incomes--compared with yours.

Last year 50 predominantly white colleges received $416,000,000 in gifts. For our 36 Negro colleges, we

Imagine you're on a train, going to your work. You make this journey daily, one hour out in the morning, another hour coming back each evening. You don't like it, but you get used to it. You pray each day you'll get a seat and when you do, you try to use your time productively. With the vagaries of modern train travel, that's no sure thing. It's simply what many have to do, day in, day out.

You have your book, your tablet and your smartphone. On the wall, or on the seat back in front of you, is a colourful poster with a simple proposition and storyline. This month it's about mosquito nets. Malaria kills a child every 45 seconds, it tells you. The solution is mosquito nets, £3.00 is all they cost and each one saves a life. Text five digits now and you can buy one, instantly, no fuss. You'll save a life in Africa.

Wow! That's something, isn't it? You have your phone; you can do it now. The cost is incidental. And for the next hour that poster will be in front of you, reminding you, gently cajoling you and castigating you too, if you don't. This is dwell time.[1]

1 Some text in this anecdote comes from *Storytelling can change the world*, by Ken Burnett, 2014

SIGNIFICANCE AND SPECIAL CHARACTERISTICS

Dwell time is not new. Back in 1968, long before campaigners and direct marketers started to get excited about the concept, David Ogilvy famously raised $26,000 in one night (a lot, back then) with a campaign promoting the United Negro College Fund that involved placing a letter on every seat of every train leaving New York's Grand Central Station. It was quite a thing for those commuters, that evening, to find a white envelope on every seat. It got their attention, right off. The name of the sender impressed them too. Then they read the letter.

BACKGROUND STORY

The United Negro College Fund is an impressive organisation. With its mottoes, 'A mind is a terrible thing to waste' and 'We can't simply believe in equality in education. We have to create it', the Fund has raised over $3billion to send 60,000 underserved black and minority ethnic students to college in the United States. That's some achievement.

Ogilvy not only understood that his travelling audience – mostly well-to-do commuters heading to their homes in the country – would have time to read that letter and might even be grateful for it. He also anticipated that if, as they read, they were to look out of their train window as it left New York they'd see directly into the run-down inner-city environments he was writing about. They'd see right inside the backyards and mean streets that the students he was exhorting them to support would be dreaming of escaping. Of course his idea would work. It was bound to. It worked brilliantly.

IMPACT, INFLUENCE AND OPPORTUNITIES

The letter is splendidly well-written, but most of all it's been carefully planned and placed. David Ogilvy knew his audience, knew they would have time on their hands and that through their journey he could show them the people he wanted them to help. Dwell time and the generosity of strangers did the rest. Very copyable.

LINKS TO MORE ON THIS CAMPAIGN

https://sofii.org/article/david-ogilvys-letter-for-the-united-negro-college-fund-from-1968

https://sofii.org/case-study/david-ogilvys-letter-for-the-united-negro-college-fund

36 Engaging supporters: Friends of the Earth, Age UK and the humble bee

WHY I CHOSE THESE

The tiny, humble bee is not beneath the concerns of the campaigning fundraiser, far from it. In fact, bees are in great danger, yet if our society is to survive and thrive, we really need them. So, who can the bees turn to for protection in their time of trouble? Why, campaigning fundraisers, of course, who in their turn unfailingly turn to their donors. Fundraisers are not averse to co-opting the bee to help them fundraise for other causes too. Well, that's only fair, isn't it? These two bee-related appeals are very different, but equally instructive.

ORIGINS AND OBJECTIVES

Gandhi once said that if you think you're too small and insignificant to make a difference, you've never spent a night alone with a mosquito. He was right – something so small and seemingly inconsequential as a bee can be

the focus of a fundraising campaign that really makes a big difference. And someone as seemingly insignificant as 91-year-old Jean Bishop can make a difference too, through engaging donors with her cause.

SIGNIFICANCE AND SPECIAL CHARACTERISTICS

Volunteers dressing up as bees are a common denominator here. The indomitable spirit of volunteers is invariably an inspiration for professionals. Volunteers remind us that our skills and professionalism are not automatically transferrable between causes, that people have to believe passionately in the cause if they're to function effectively as a real donor or as a fundraiser, that the professional campaigning fundraiser can never be cause agnostic.

BACKGROUND STORY

The ask from Friends of the Earth is twofold. First, visitors to their website are asked to sign a petition requesting the UK's prime minister for a 'bee action' plan to save British bees. Second, FoE requests that supporters donate £15 to help save bees. In return, donors receive a 'bee saver' pack, which includes wildflower seeds, a guide to identifying and saving bees and a garden planner.

Jean's story is a bit different. Wearing her homemade bee costume, she will frequently be found outside her local shopping centre, raising much-needed funds for Age UK. Street fundraising is often unpopular, but Jean has managed to earn the public's love. She's also collected a staggering £110,000. Jean makes a note of everything she raises in her little book. The day she reached her initial goal of £100,000 Joan wrote 'start again'. She is truly unstoppable. 'They call me the bee lady,' says Jean, with modesty and considerable pride. 'When I put on my costume, I become the bee. I am the bee!' Exuberantly, Jean explains that the bee only has two rules: 'Number one,' she says, 'always have a smile for everyone you meet. And number two, never ever shake your tin.'

IMPACT, INFLUENCE AND OPPORTUNITIES

Apart from the bees loving both campaigns on sight, charity staff and supporters of all ages fell headlong for them too. And the campaigning fundraisers, well, what could be better? So, it's win, win, win for the bees.

LINKS TO MORE ON THESE CAMPAIGNS

https://sofii.org/case-study/friends-of-the-earth-the-bee-cause
https://sofii.org/article/becoming-the-bee-with-jean-bishop

37 The very moving image: how DRTV came to the aid of fundraising

WHY I CHOSE THIS

As you watch the first of these selected advertisements, as the camera leads you through the dark, dismal room, I dare you to look into little Ellie's eyes at the point when her fear turns slowly into the biggest of smiles, and not be moved from terror to jubilation. If campaigning fundraisers would master the prudent use of emotion, sometimes only sound and vision will do, as these ads all show. The NSPCC's Ellie ad stopped viewers in their tracks, whatever they were doing. Do watch it. Though dated now its appeal is still irresistible, as great fundraising should always be. This is DRTV – direct response television – at its finest.

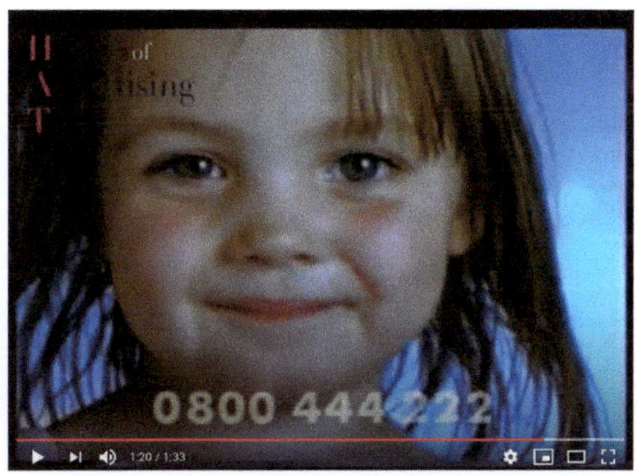

ORIGINS AND OBJECTIVES

The entry fee for TV advertising is expensive, though for cost per viewer it can be comparatively cheap. Yet until quite recently the cost of TV advertising was considered entirely prohibitive by most charities. Now we know, as with radio, DRTV is one of the most cost-effective of media for the campaigning fundraiser. The story behind this realisation is worth knowing, and examples of where it's done really well are well worth studying too.

SIGNIFICANCE AND SPECIAL CHARACTERISTICS

Short of being there in person, nothing is so powerful as the sound and vision of film. Here we feature just four, from a very instructive body of work.

BACKGROUND STORY

How NSPCC's Ellie ad popularised TV use by charities in the UK and the story of the creative collaboration between NSPCC's Giles Pegram and direct marketing supremo John Watson is told in the links below. Also, there's an uplifting comment on the ad from writer Indra Sinha. Unmissable. Some years later RSPCA's seasonal good wishes led the way with a new approach, a great charity ad that shows the power of simple emotional storytelling, with no request for funds at all. The MS Society in Holland also uses emotion brilliantly, yet not a single word is spoken. In a longer infomercial Jiblu, for Islamic Relief, makes us laugh while showing that delivering aid internationally isn't quite as easy as it might seem.

IMPACT, INFLUENCE AND OPPORTUNITIES

The NSPCC ad opened the floodgates, making DRTV a fundraising staple. Since then, the variety and creativity of campaigning fundraising DRTV ads have been unceasing. Yet many causes still feel excluded because TV advertising unquestionably calls for bigger budgets than most charities can generally deploy. We're all familiar with TV advertisers' annual pre-Christmas scramble for customers and the dominance of high-budget, emotional storytelling ads on our screens from the nation's best-known supermarkets, each vying to compete with each other to present the most emotional seasonal campaign. Pre-Christmas, as we all know only too well, is also the most productive time for fundraisers. So why – with a few notable exceptions – is this time on TV the exclusive territory of

supermarkets and their likes and not a fertile field for charities and their campaigning fundraisers? Is this not a chance for collaboration, for pooled effort to take on the annual Christmas TV ads phenomenon? I think it is, and a great opportunity awaits those charities that can crack it.

Campaigning fundraisers could also be making much better use of short amateur videos than they routinely do. We now all have a mobile movie camera in our pockets and handbags. Shooting video is easy (shooting great video much more difficult, of course. But we shouldn't let the perfect get in the way of what we know will work, should we?). Short videos in on-line appeals and thank-you emails can be delightful for donors.

> **'…for example, charity:water sent a short and sweet thank-you email with a prominent "Watch the video >>" button. It took me to a delightful thank you video that immersed me – sight and sound – in the great good my gift was poised to achieve. I felt connected, glad, part of something bigger than myself, and all in less than a minute or two.'**
>
> Lisa Sargent, *Thankology*, to be published later in 2021

LINKS TO MORE ON THE MOVING IMAGE

https://sofii.org/article/the-use-and-misuse-of-emotion-part-one
https://sofii.org/article/the-use-and-misuse-of-emotion-part-two
https://sofii.org/case-study/first-successful-drtv-ad-in-the-uk-ellie
https://www.youtube.com/watch?v=CLoaq2IsScI
https://sofii.org/case-study/multiple-sclerosis-society-holland-television-commercial
https://sofii.org/case-study/islamic-relief-saving-lives-isnt-easy-video

38 Building support: Durham Cathedral in LEGO

WHY I CHOSE THIS

Buy-a-brick fundraising appeals are almost as old as bricks themselves. LEGO bricks of course are more recent arrivals. Creating an exact replica of this stunning Cathedral was an inspired involvement initiative that raised over £300,000 and had many spin-off benefits too.

ORIGINS AND OBJECTIVES

Durham Cathedral in LEGO was devised as a fundraising project to raise funds to finance the Cathedral's world-class exhibition experience 'Open Treasure'.

SIGNIFICANCE AND SPECIAL CHARACTERISTICS

A classic case history of donor involvement, the building in LEGO captured imaginations and attracted much attention. The symbolism of building the Cathedral in LEGO brick by brick enabled sponsors and donors to see and imagine the difference their gifts made possible. Tee-shirts, mugs and even limited-edition mini models were sold far and wide. After three years of the engaging, involving fundraising that it took to complete the huge and complex model, the final brick could at last be put carefully into place. Over 40,000 people tuned in to watch that last brick being added through a live Facebook stream.

BACKGROUND STORY

In return for a donation of £1.00, members of the public were invited to buy a LEGO brick that they could personally add to a scale model of the Cathedral. The model attracted interest from visitors across the world and inspired local community groups and businesses to support the Cathedral by building sections of the model. Seven-year-old Pearl Richardson, whose father is a stonemason working at the Cathedral, won a prize draw for the honour of laying the final brick. The LEGO cathedral currently holds the record for the largest LEGO model built by ordinary people. With 300,000 bricks and 1,450 individual modules, it is 5ft 6in (1.7m) high, 12ft 6in (3.84m) long and 5ft (1.53m) wide. The accurate scale model includes altars, crosses, arched windows, gargoyles and stained glass.

IMPACT, INFLUENCE AND OPPORTUNITIES

Five short films were created to tell the story of Durham Cathedral in LEGO from the life of St Cuthbert to Cathedral life today. Viewed over 50,000 times in just five weeks, the films engaged new audiences and promoted the 'Open Treasure' exhibition. The campaign won a major award at the UK Institute of Fundraising awards (sponsored by SOFII) and inspired similar fundraising initiatives too.

Sometimes the simplest, most traditional forms of fundraising are the best. I don't know whether the fundraisers erected a huge thermometer outside the Cathedral's door, but why not? Here's something tangible, very visible, involving, beautiful, useful and fun to get involved in. What's not to love?

> **'I visited a couple of years ago with fellow students from my stained-glass class and we couldn't resist the opportunity to buy enough transparent coloured glass bricks to make our own little window for the model.'**
>
> Susan Langford, Cathedral visitor

LINK TO MORE ON THIS CAMPAIGN

https://sofii.org/case-study/durham-cathedral-in-lego-innovative-buy-a-brick-fundraising

39 Creative plagiarism: CPAR Ethiopia creates a fundraising first

WHY I CHOSE THIS

What must it be like to launch the first ever public appeal in a whole country? Particularly if that country is one of the world's poorest and the results you get are, well, quite frankly phenomenal.

CPAR ETHIOPIA

Plant a Tree in Ethiopia

CPAR's innovative new campaign to help preserve our environment

July 1997

Dear

One of our greatest pleasures when we were kids was joining our fathers for forest fruit collection and hunting. Together we would flounder in the thick forests listening to the call of the beautiful music of the forest creatures.

We are ashamed to admit it, but today we can't introduce our grandchildren to the same pleasures. In many places, the trees and forests of our countryside have been completely cleared, not withstanding one generation's greed, and therefore denying future generations of their basic needs. Needs such as clean air, drinkable water, productive land, clothing and shelter.

Fortunately, there are people in our community who have recognized the dangers of deforestation, making it possible to reverse the process.

ORIGINS AND OBJECTIVES

That's what a really sharp Italian woman called Nadia Weber did when she decided to raise funds in Ethiopia for the local branch of the non-profit Canadian Physicians for Aid and Relief (CPAR). She'd never done direct mail fundraising before, but she decided that was the fundraising method she wanted to employ, so she set about learning all she could about the medium then copied the best she could find from other practitioners. The result is a remarkably competent communication that would have done well in any market.

SIGNIFICANCE AND SPECIAL CHARACTERISTICS

The vivid picture of need that Nadia creates in this letter is irresistible. Her choice of language – the use of words and phrases such as 'floundering in the forest' – is charming and compelling. The direct mail package she went on to produce is a lesson in creative plagiarism – borrowing the best of others, then adding to it. But the most unusual feature of this appeal is who she chose to send it to and how well it worked – she mailed the Addis Ababa telephone directory.

BACKGROUND STORY

I was alerted to this story by fundraising legend and fellow countryman of mine Bernard Ross, and first wrote it up as a case history for my 2006 book *The Zen of Fundraising*. Everything about the story is great, but the bit I particularly loved was that in his half-hour lightning tour of direct mail fundraising Bernard had neglected to tell Nadia what levels of response to expect. That first mailing brought in a response of 40 per cent. Extraordinary, yet Nadia was devastated. What, she worried, had happened to the other 60 per cent?

IMPACT, INFLUENCE AND OPPORTUNITIES

What had happened to the others, indeed? We should be told. Apart from the fact that a five per cent response to a cold mail appeal would be considered exceptionally good by most seasoned fundraisers. This brilliant inspiration for creative world-changers everywhere shows the scope for initiative that can be found if you approach the task of campaigning fundraising in a positive way.

To succeed in this competitive world, campaigning fundraisers need to be enterprising, aware, imaginative, learned, skilful and courageous. They'll also need to take risks and, at times, to take a leap in the dark – provided they've first done their homework and prepared all they can. This initiative shows yet another example of how such creative risk-taking can pay off. So, why are so many charities so timid and risk-averse? Or are they simply unaware?

LINK TO MORE ON THIS CAMPAIGN

https://sofii.org/case-study/cpar-plant-a-tree-in-ethiopia-mailing

40 **Beautiful *and* effective:** RSPB's brand stretch and letter to the future

WHY I CHOSE THIS

In a glittering array of beautiful moments, the Royal Society for the Protection of Birds (RSPB) presented stunning pictures and uplifting messages to create a fresh, striking image of their core product and proposition for a range of audiences, new and old. Then, on an issue of national importance, RSPB invited all their supporters to sign and send a letter designed to change government policy, for good.

ORIGINS AND OBJECTIVES

Already enjoying a distinctive, hugely respected identity RSPB's purpose was to increase their influence on government policy, to recruit new members and to stretch their brand to enhance its personality and appeal, thereby increasing its attractiveness to the widest possible group of supporters as a prelude to mobilising them towards effecting lasting political change.

SIGNIFICANCE AND SPECIAL CHARACTERISTICS

Campaigning organisations can regularly employ lofty ideals, universal values and iconic imagery to propel their messages and achieve impact. It pays also to talk with supporters, not at them. All these came together in these two classic campaigns, which must have been the best fun to work on. It helped that RSPB's photo library holds some of the most stunning images to be found anywhere.

Branding campaigns from charities are often ineffective, at times expensive, wasteful and misguided. I've already criticised awareness ads (see exhibit 21) and agree with Mark Phillips when he says, 'Branding has given us some of the biggest problems that we face in fundraising. Awareness campaigns that say, "look at us, aren't we great?" have diminished the value of the voluntary sector and confused donors.'

'The brands they [commercial companies] create for the products and services they sell normally have a guarantee at their core. It says, "we are great because you can depend on our product to wash your clothes whiter, make you better looking, appear cooler, give you more energy, make you thinner, or whatever the consumer hands over their money for".
'And that doesn't transfer to charities. A charity actually has to say something completely different.
'They have to say, "we depend on you".'

Mark Phillips, writing in the Queer Ideas blog, linked below.

That said, when done well and tailored to the specific needs of campaigning fundraisers, branding campaigns can be impressive, especially if accompanied by an explicit, measurable objective. This is one such example.

BACKGROUND STORY

RSPB has more than a million members and a prominent, commanding position on anything to do with wild birds. These exhibits show that the impact of their work is a lot wider than just the protection of birds, that RSPB is a very elastic brand, capable of appealing to just about everyone, not just dedicated birdwatchers.

IMPACT, INFLUENCE AND OPPORTUNITIES

The posters alone present a masterclass in the brilliant combination of verbal imagery and great photographs. But there's much more here. These images unlock the imagination, make hearts soar and literally raise a million voices for nature. Any campaigning fundraiser who doesn't look at these and say, 'Wow, I wish I'd thought of that', probably is being economical with the truth.

This is a multi-channel campaign with shared values at its centre. As IWITOT Toronto speaker Taslim Somani described, it's bold, big-picture and about the brand, a fundraising campaign but with no fundraising ask. It appeals to the universal love of and belief in nature and it asks for a campaigning action. Nearly 400,000 people signed RSPB's letter to the future.

Brave and risky, yes. Effective, sure. We should see more like this. There must be opportunities galore for fundraisers on the likes of Instagram. Ryan Burdock, who's much younger than I so more comfortable with such things, told me that billions of images are viewed on Instagram every day, but as yet there's no outstanding fundraising appeal via image. Seems like an opening to me, too.

LINKS TO MORE ON THESE CAMPAIGNS

https://sofii.org/case-study/rspb-brand-stretch-work

https://sofii.org/case-study/rspbs-letter-to-the-future

https://queerideas.co.uk/2010/06/why-i-love-branding.html

41 'Why us?': ActionAid reinvents the loose insert for new donor recruitment

WHY I CHOSE THIS

What do you do when you're already using all available media so effectively that merely increasing your appearances simply dilutes results, yet suddenly you need to find lots more supporters quickly and cost-effectively to meet your obligations to beneficiaries? You reinvent your use of media and change how you present your proposition, that's what.

ORIGINS AND OBJECTIVES

ActionAid was a tiny charity in the late 1970s/early 80s, but it was already gaining a reputation for its sure-footed use of direct marketing to recruit monthly donors onto its child sponsorship scheme. Then, a commitment to bring education to 2,000 children in Southern India presented ActionAid with the above dilemma.

SIGNIFICANCE AND SPECIAL CHARACTERISTICS

Like ActionAid, many charities at the time could still use press advertising cost-effectively, but there were clear signs that the heyday of 'off-the-page' was already past. Media costs had escalated, readership and responses were falling, the cost of acquisition for most advertisers was nearing prohibitive. As happens every so often (see exhibit 31), a new method of supporter acquisition was needed.

BACKGROUND STORY

This problem arose just as ActionAid's main banker media, *The Sunday Times* and *The Observer* colour magazines, were both considering accepting loose inserts for the first time. But though they are delivered to the same potential readership, inserts cost many times more than a whole page ad to print and insert, so they have to work that much harder, for the extra cost to be justified. ActionAid knew a long copy story would work, but it was a massive risk for a small budget. How could they guarantee success? Then a print rep from a New Jersey-based specialist printer asked if he could come and present a new print format. It was a simple four-page leaflet, but new in-line finishing technology now enabled the printing of a ready gummed, perforated reply envelope and coupon that folds in (see left-hand panel in the example overleaf) from the fore-edge of page 3. I was heading

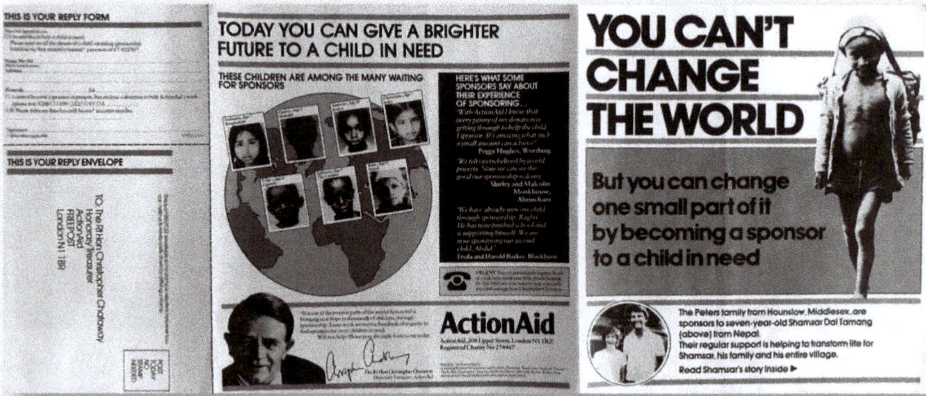

ActionAid's fundraising at the time. Soon as I saw it, I realised ActionAid had to have it. Though subsequently commonplace, at the time nothing like it had ever been seen before.

IMPACT, INFLUENCE AND OPPORTUNITIES

From the insert's first appearance ActionAid recruited more than 1,000 new regular donors significantly more cheaply than traditional ads. A new format was launched that, for a while, enjoyed spectacular success before it too began to suffer from over-familiarity. Copied by many, ActionAid alone produced tens of millions of these inserts each year in a variety of sizes and formats. Structured tests (the beauty of the loose insert is that it affords multiple test opportunities) showed ActionAid that their innovative built-in reply device justified its additional marginal cost. Thus, the once derided loose insert enjoyed a new, albeit brief, lease of life and ActionAid's rapid growth accelerated.

Something was nagging at me as that print rep left my office clutching his first order for this revolutionary new technology. So, I stopped him at the door with an obvious question. 'Why us?', I asked. 'Why are you giving this new opportunity to a piddling little newcomer like ActionAid and not to one of the big fundraising charities?' The printer looked very depressed. 'Simple,' he said. 'You're the only person who has given me a hearing. I contacted all the big charities, but they were all too busy to even see me.'

In meetings, I expect. Poor them.

LINK TO MORE ON THIS INNOVATION

https://sofii.org/case-study/the-actionaid-inserts-with-built-in-reply-mechanism

42 Political campaigning and fundraising: Common Cause and the birth of citizen advocacy

WHY I CHOSE THIS

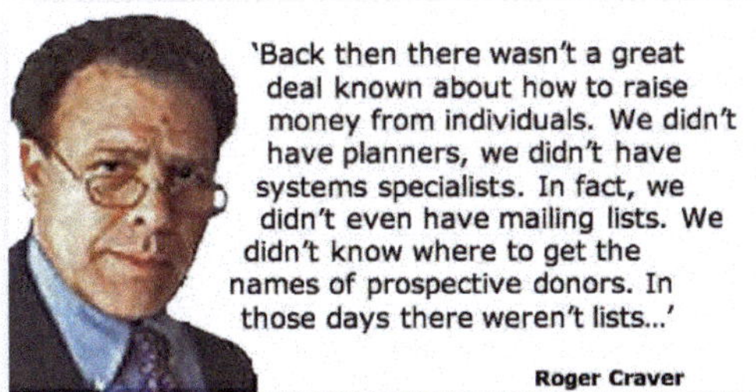

From even before the campaign to abolish the slave trade it's never been possible to cleanly separate politics from fundraising. This is true in just about every country, despite sustained efforts to regulate and curb fundraising charities' potential to involve themselves in 'political actions'. As we've seen, charities can't separate campaigning from fundraising. Yet all campaigning for change is essentially political, so it's a considerable grey area for charities, as can be seen in RSPB's letter to the future (exhibit 40), Nazis against Nazis (exhibit 33) and countless other charity campaigns. As sub-genres go, political fundraising is worth studying more than most.

ORIGINS AND OBJECTIVES

Political fundraising's most experienced aficionado in the USA is Roger Craver, aka the Agitator, a key figure in the civil rights movement of the 1960s and 70s and writer of this book's foreword. Roger shaped political fundraising for the modern era and is still agitating for and advising political groups to this day. He was one of Common Cause's founders, providing early evidence that campaigning fundraisers can and do lead change.

It's hard to believe that in 1970s America, women could not get their own credit cards when they graduated from school unless their husband or father was willing to sign for it. In the USA Common Cause has fought successfully for major reforms. With nearly 400,000 members and supporters and 36 state organisations, Common Cause remains committed to honest, open and accountable government, as well as encouraging citizen participation in democracy. The advertisement overleaf is based on one of the most famous response ads of all time, from the legendary John Caples (see exhibit 21).

SIGNIFICANCE AND SPECIAL CHARACTERISTICS

Different jurisdictions have differing rules. In the UK, to be a charity an organisation must be established for charitable purposes only, which are

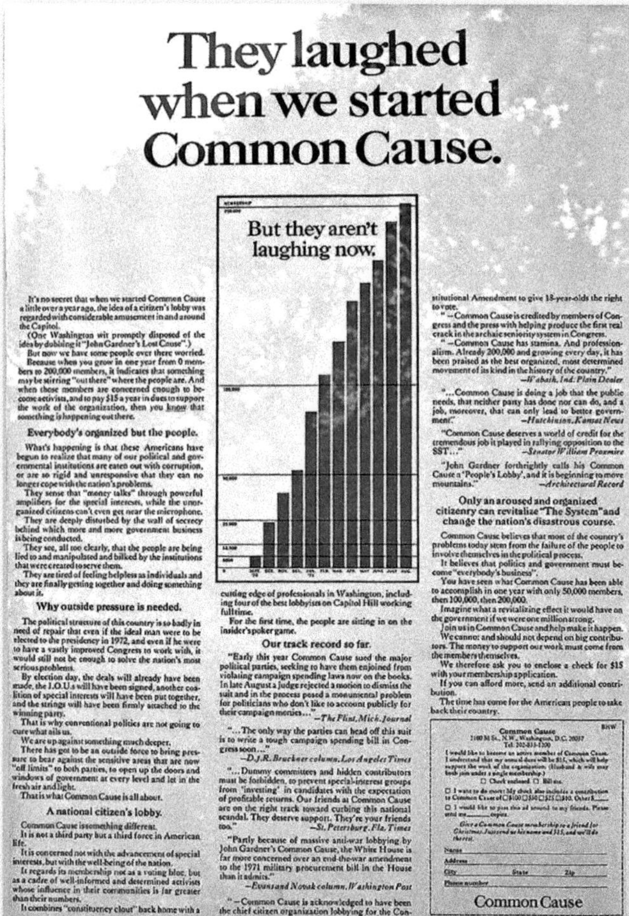

for the public benefit. An organisation will not be charitable if its purposes are political. Paradoxically though, campaigning and political activity can be legitimate and valuable activities for charities to undertake. Amnesty's ads featured in exhibit 26 changed the face of political campaigning in the UK. Still, Greenpeace, Amnesty and others eschew charitable registration for their political activities, preferring the relative freedom to campaign that limited company status provides. In reality most charities are inevitably political and have to be if they wish to change society. So the division is unclear, outdated and unhelpful, thus it remains incumbent on campaigning charities to push the boundaries and even to campaign for the distinction to be abolished so that charities can be allowed to agitate for the changes they wish to see, without restrictions.

BACKGROUND STORY

'Anyone who thinks money doesn't buy an election is insane.' So tweeted a political pundit in the run-up to the USA's 2020 presidential election. Reforming the financing of political campaigns has traditionally been a priority for Common Cause, because it believes that the undue influence of big money in politics undermines the public's interest. Common Cause was the first political advocacy organisation to prove that you could attract tens of millions of dollars in small – $10, $15 – amounts. It was out of Common Cause that the example grew for the founding of organisations like the National Organization for Women, the Environmental Defense Fund and Greenpeace, all of which Roger Craver helped to organise in the late 1960s and early 1970s. As Roger says, 'you have to keep fighting for these "rights" issues, because even when you win, these battles never stay won'. So, pushing the boundaries comes with the territory for political fundraisers.

IMPACT, INFLUENCE AND OPPORTUNITIES

If you want to be heard, you've got to make a noise. With almost daily emails to donors at the height of campaigning, political fundraising is undeniably instructive for its sheer scale, lofty rhetoric, intense frequency and generally brilliant use of data.

LINKS TO MORE ON POLITICAL CAMPAIGNING AND FUNDRAISING

https://sofii.org/case-study/the-society-for-effecting-the-abolition-of-the-slave-trade-minute-regarding-the-need-for-fundraising-from-1788
https://sofii.org/case-study/common-cause-the-birth-of-modern-citizen-advocacy
https://sofii.org/article/still-in-the-battle-an-interview-with-roger-craver
https://sofii.org/case-study/common-cause-citizens-committee-major-donor-upgrade
https://sofii.org/case-study/pete-for-america-leaderboard-challenge-election-fundraising

HOW THE AGITATOR SEES IT:

http://agitator.thedonorvoice.com/american-renewal

43 Shopping lists: £5.00 buys a pair of sturdy boots that someone you'll never know might rely on, as he or she saves you

WHY I CHOSE THIS

If mastery of emotion is the storyteller's most powerful asset it's the shopping list that's ubiquitous in encouraging donors to choose their comfortable giving level and where they'd most like their gift to be directed.

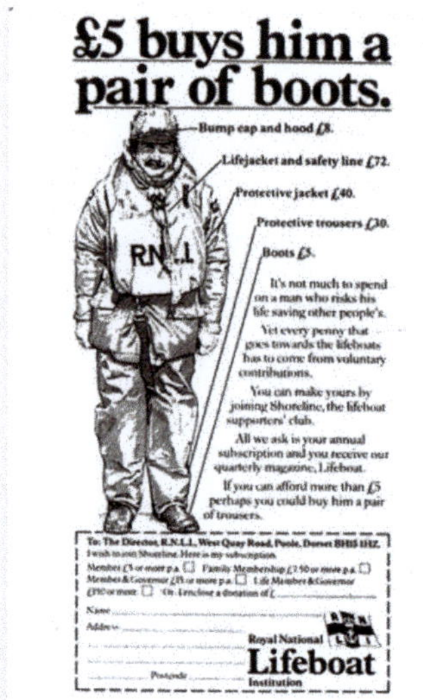

A classic example of the 'shopping-list' approach from RNLI.

ORIGINS AND OBJECTIVES

Use of the once universal shopping list or similar variants goes back hundreds of years, though its actual origins are as yet unknown. The shopping list's success rests on its intelligent price structure and the natural human desire to know what their gift will buy. What tangible, urgent, evident need can I as a donor readily afford to fill? Present me with a choice and your success is assured. Actually, though, tell me where I too could buy boots of seagoing quality for just £5.00 and I'll double my donation. (I know the ad above appeared a while ago, but, really!...) A key to success for any business is getting the pricing right. Charities are no exception.

SIGNIFICANCE AND SPECIAL CHARACTERISTICS

Items selected for shopping lists must be readily imaginable, appropriately priced, practical, appealing and true. But it should be clear they're examples of what your gift might buy, not what your gift will buy.

BACKGROUND STORY

Donors can't get enough of shopping lists because crucial to their giving is knowing how much they should give and what their donation might be used for. The best place to put your shopping list is on the reply form itself (though you should test this, of course). It's also a good idea to present an affordable range, including one or two that might stretch the average donor (without overt influencing, of course, so the donor retains control over his or her choice. Many donors see donation strings as subliminal manipulation, so it pays to be careful). And it can be worthwhile to include something very general, such as, 'Wherever the need is greatest' (see also exhibit 6). While everyone likes the ability to choose, some donors prefer the choice to be made for them. If a donor trusts you enough to send a gift, chances are he or she will also trust you to choose where it should be applied.

IMPACT, INFLUENCE AND OPPORTUNITIES

A Cancer Research UK campaign featured at IWITOT for Stand up to Cancer was almost entirely built upon weird and whacky shopping list items. In praising the campaign's donation rewards menu its presenter Andy McSorley said,

> **'I wish I'd thought of this because it works. It changes the state of play. It puts the donor experience at the forefront of a campaign in a completely unique way. It could also be a platform for a tonal shift in fundraising language.'**

Proof you can even have fun with shopping lists. I've no direct evidence to back my feeling that the shopping list has fallen from favour with fundraisers of late, but I fear it has just because I see it less often. I doubt that fundraising will work better without it. And I suspect that its omission is unlikely ever to have been tested.

LINKS TO MORE ON SHOPPING LISTS

https://sofii.org/case-study/royal-national-lifeboat-institution-boots-advertisement

https://sofii.org/article/stand-up-to-cancer-2018

PART 5

The culture of campaigning fundraising

No other business area is remotely like the fundraising sector. Imagine! Supporters differ fundamentally from customers, they have motives, passions and emotions a world away from the self-interest that usually underpins a purchase. Most voluntary sector income comes in the form of gifts given freely, no strings attached, with no tangible goods or service provided in return. Campaigning fundraisers attract gifts in support from sometimes wealthy, sometimes hard-pressed but always well-motivated, inspired individuals. Many if not most of their biggest donations come in the form of legacies from the recently deceased, or from gifts given in memory of someone no longer living. They sell recycled goods in shops where the majority of things sold are donated, they organise huge public events of endless variety where the giving of time is as valuable and valued as the giving of money, touching just about anyone with a warm and generous heart. All in the name of thousands of good and great causes, each designed specifically to make the world a better place. And we're only just beginning to understand the power and potential in the warm good feeling that this support generates among the givers.

The campaigning fundraising sector is special indeed. Its distinctiveness is marked out by the fundamental principles we've already seen illustrated in part 1 (see page 28) and also by the cultural pillars set out here, in these final nine exhibits of part 5.

Many of the issues highlighted here – leadership, investment, storytelling – will of course be found in other fields of business, though perhaps with a different nature, emphasis and spin. But equally, some of the other issues featured here – the use and misuse of emotion, working together, helping each other and the appliance of new areas of science – are all exclusive to campaigning fundraisers or at least idiosyncratically different in their impact and effects. They reflect the uniquely distinctive culture that our varied publics all like to see firmly enshrined at the core of not-for-profit or for-change sector organisations everywhere.

Part 5 celebrates what should be that difference and distinctiveness.

44 Investment in fundraising: the vital need for sustained and sufficient spending

WHY I CHOSE THIS

Few investments deliver better returns more reliably than prudent spending on the generation of income for fundraising organisations. Yet for some inexplicable reason even the mere mention of the word investment seems enough to cause trustee boards to run for cover or head for the hills.

ORIGINS AND OBJECTIVES

A version of the chart shown here was initially commissioned by Giles Pegram CBE when he was head of fundraising at NSPCC, because he wanted an easy way to show how a charity could get spectacularly better results from investing in fundraising rather than, as is commonplace for charities, investing their reserves in stocks, shares and bonds. The chart shows that if fundraisers can keep their nerve during the initial investment phase the return on investment in acquiring new donors quickly and reliably outstrips just about any other practical investment – outperforming the traditional returns from stocks, bonds and shares by three or four times, or more.

SIGNIFICANCE AND SPECIAL CHARACTERISTICS

It's an obvious no brainer and something of a scandal that this is not better understood by senior management teams and trustee boards. Almost all charities keep the best part of their reserves invested in the financial markets, which generally perform poorly, while far too many neglect to invest adequately or sensibly in their own acquisition and development of donors. This truth is a constant source of despair and derision from fundraising consultants, even though this example of trustee ineptness keeps them comfortably in business.

BACKGROUND STORY

Despite the immense value it would bring and the undeniable fact that most charities are only too willing to share their secrets, there's still no sound, robust system for collecting and sharing response data on fundraising RoI (return on investment) and donor lifetime values that would make the figures in the chart opposite impossible to ignore or deny. Aversion to investment in fundraising is really incomprehensible,

WHY EXPENDITURE ON FUNDRAISING SHOULD BE SEEN AS AN INVESTMENT, NOT A COST

How fundraising investment works

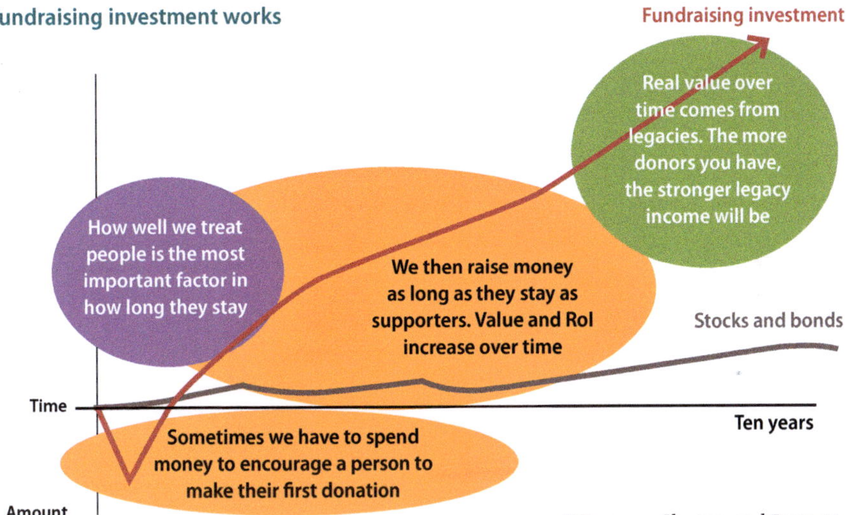

© Pegram, Clayton and Burnett

THE SAME CHART VIEWED SLIGHTLY DIFFERENTLY

Let's say a charity takes £1 million from reserves...

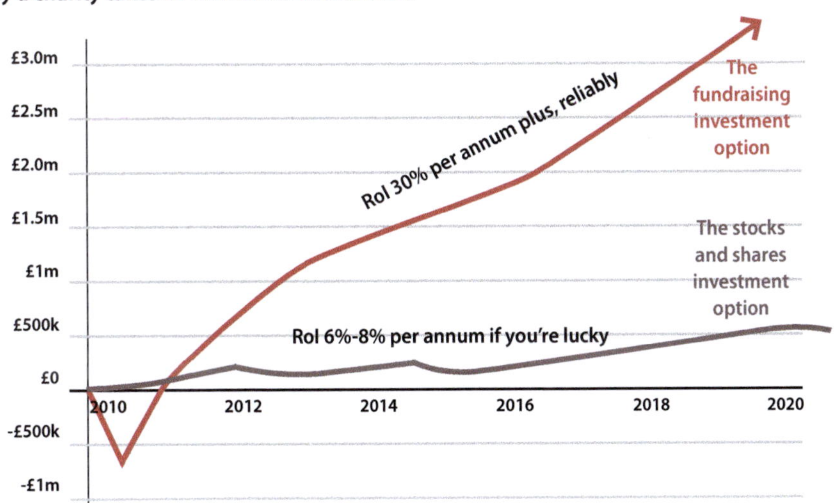

among charities. Of course we have to be careful with charitable funds; we must abhor waste and seek optimum value for money, but we all know cheapest is seldom best and in this business area false economies abound. Cheeseparing costs the charity sector massively, particularly its persistent underinvestment in people and their training. The high turnover of fundraisers is just one telling by-product. And investment in donor acquisition and development – if done properly – is about as safe and guaranteed as any investment gets. These issues must be grasped now, as the new era of responsible fundraising evolves.

> **'Donors do not come first. Fundraisers come first. If you take care of your fundraisers, they will take care of your donors.'**
>
> Paraphrased from a comment by Richard Branson, entrepreneur and billionaire

IMPACT, INFLUENCE AND OPPORTUNITIES

Those causes that have invested wisely have invariably prospered. But there's none so blind as those that will not see.

> **'Fundraising is an area which really does flourish when given the time, skills, and resources. Charities that succeed over the long term will be the ones that invest in their fundraising – and not solely in financial terms – this could be investment in skills, people, systems, or activity.'**
>
> Daniel Fluskey, head of policy and external affairs, Chartered Institute of Fundraising, UK

There's a need for collective, concerted action to communicate this across our entire sector. The reason we fail to get this across is that everyone hopes that the other organisation will take the risk of standing above the parapet to shout about it. So please, copy the charts on page 159 and circulate them to your senior management team and board of trustees. Make sure they understand the issue and can access case histories of organisations that have demonstrated it.

> **'Now [during the coronavirus pandemic] is the time to be eagle-eyed on cancellations and delinquencies and have a plan to reach out and offer to pause or renegotiate their giving…**

'...low interest rates (cheap money) represent a historic opportunity for non-profits. If ever there was a time to substantially boost acquisition investment and increase spend on donor care and improving donor experience now is the moment. The financially wise non-profit will seize this opportunity for both new donor growth and to invest in hiking retention rates.

'Of course, it's highly unlikely that most boards, CEOs or even CFOs will think this way. Conventional wisdom, as best as I can tell, is that in the midst of this uncertainty and economic recession "we should pull back" ..."husband our resources" ..."not be aggressive at a time like this"...and a thousand other cautionary excuses.'

The Agitator, The Cheap Money Paradox, 23 September 2020

Too many charities focus on short-term RoI and not enough on the longer-term measure that is lifetime value (LTV). Most experts and pundits in the for-change sector, when they talk about lifetime value are referring to the total value to the cause in funds raised from a specific donor. That's crucial to know, of course. Sadly they're not yet thinking in terms of lifetime value *for the donor*, the value he or she will derive from a lifetime of being a supporter. Campaigning fundraisers will profit for sure if they can learn to define and communicate that durable, substantial, desirable value. This is the core of the CIoF's Supporter Experience Project, and while this focus is an aspect still largely unexplored by academics and researchers, that will change dramatically, quite soon.

LINKS TO MORE ON INVESTMENT IN FUNDRAISING

https://sofii.org/cde/the-commission-on-the-donor-experience
https://sofii.org/article/cde-project-15-summary-the-role-of-trustee-boards-and-senior-managers
https://sofii.org/cde/cde-project-20-fundraising-investment

HOW THE AGITATOR SEES IT:

http://agitator.thedonorvoice.com/the-board-meeting-swipe-file-fundraising-costs-and-investment

45 The use and misuse of emotion: CDE project 6 and its 40+ components

WHY I CHOSE THIS

Fundraising is inevitably emotional, and emotion is hugely powerful, so must be used responsibly and wisely. By definition therefore, mastery of all aspects of emotion and its communication should be mandatory for campaigning fundraisers. It isn't. And changing this will be far from easy.

ORIGINS AND OBJECTIVES

It's long been obvious to me, as a campaigning fundraiser, that I don't know enough about the massive, complex and crucial subject that is the use – and misuse – of emotion in fundraising. So, I volunteered to take responsibility for producing the Commission on the Donor Experience (CDE)'s project 6 on this theme and in the process, I learned a lot. Yet still, I only scratched the surface.

CDE project 6
Emotion

SIGNIFICANCE AND SPECIAL CHARACTERISTICS

To understand emotion and how we should use it we need to intimately understand the functioning of the human brain. Though emotions and how and why the brain works are beyond complicated, emotional fundraising isn't rocket science. Or at least, it shouldn't be regarded as such.

BACKGROUND STORY

Giving, we know, is neither logical nor rational. The almost entirely irrational decision to give is invariably first and foremost an emotional decision. And emotions are far more powerful and faster than logic – many hundreds of times faster, as it happens. CDE's project 6 set out to equip fundraisers everywhere with a broad understanding of emotions, their importance, power and potential, plus to offer practical guidance on how to access and employ them wisely and responsibly in their fundraising, to enhance their donors' experiences.

Francesco Ambrogetti, author of *Emotionraising* and *Hooked on a Feeling* and a stalwart of CDE6, says, 'When emotions like anger or fear are at play, driven by a story...they are so strong that people respond with donations in minutes and expect to see their donations at work immediately, like a dollar transforming itself instantly and magically into justice or help.'

'What's tragic,' says Francesco, 'is that before they respond and act, donors first need to see the fire from a blazing Notre-Dame, or suffering koalas or the killing of another African American in the US. As they've already been told there's a need, why can't donors just donate a month or even a year before a crisis or an accident happens?'

It's a good, even existential question. Campaigning fundraisers try to answer it with their regular giving schemes (see exhibit 19) with some success. But it's an ongoing challenge. As funders have found again and again, take the emotion out, try to get donors to think rationally about their giving and fundraising almost invariably fails.

IMPACT, INFLUENCE AND OPPORTUNITIES

For the impact and influence of emotional fundraising to grow and flourish, every campaigning fundraiser should, at the very least, set out to gain a basic understanding of this subject.

Thankfully our knowledge of the use and misuse of emotion is expanding all the time, particularly because of fresh insights from the recently arrived behavioural scientists. And there could hardly be a more important field of study for campaigning fundraisers. As it's something we as yet only partially understand, clearly we need to give it more attention. This project from CDE was merely intended to start the process. Young people coming into this sector will take this subject forward, with startling results, I'm sure.

LINKS TO MORE ON THE USE AND MISUSE OF EMOTION

https://sofii.org/cde/cde-project-6-the-use-and-misuse-of-emotion

https://sofii.org/article/cde-project-6-index-page

HOW THE AGITATOR SEES IT:

http://agitator.thedonorvoice.com/emotion-and-fundraising-will-any-emotion-do

46 The power of words: communication and the English language

WHY I CHOSE THIS

Because it illustrates why communication is the campaigning fundraiser's most important skill. And shows how staleness of imagery and lack of verbal precision – as Orwell put it – are holding fundraising back.

ORIGINS AND OBJECTIVES

Righting wrongs is what campaigning fundraisers should do routinely. Writing wrongs are more likely what you'll find. Yet written and verbal communication skills should be bread and butter to serious fundraising, for they're so necessary if we wish to spread inspiration. No exaggeration, communication skills should be the key thing employers look for when recruiting their campaigning fundraisers.

SIGNIFICANCE AND SPECIAL CHARACTERISTICS

Writing in 1946, social critic and author George Orwell expressed the belief, 'that prose consists less and less of words chosen for the sake of their meaning, and more and more of phrases tacked together like the sections of a prefabricated hen-house'. Nice image! Perhaps this problem has ever been with us, but I venture to suggest it's getting worse. For all the reasons Orwell understood so well, communication via the written word falls far short, far too often. For campaigning fundraisers, this won't do at all, because it's our primary means of reaching our constituents.

BACKGROUND STORY

We campaigning fundraisers have the best stories in the world to tell and the best of reasons for telling them with power and passion that will move people to action. So why, when fundraisers write up their work to present it to their various publics, why do they so often make the resulting verbiage dull, impenetrable, jargon-ridden and hard to comprehend? Campaigning fundraisers should realise that words are precision instruments capable of taking us directly to the hearts of our donors. Most of our communications with potential supporters are written, so we should deploy our words with great care and clear understanding of their meaning and impact.

We have a choice when we sit down to write – to write something that might make a difference or to write something that will make no difference at all. We wouldn't choose the latter deliberately, so our lack of success must be down to carelessness, or ignorance, or a failure to appreciate the importance of it. Every day we all use words to communicate what we want to get across, in a range of ways. Our success or failure at it really matters. And mostly, most of us don't manage to do it very well.

IMPACT, INFLUENCE AND OPPORTUNITIES

'...apart from avoidable ugliness, two qualities are common. The first is staleness of imagery; the other is lack of precision. The writer either has a meaning and cannot express it, or he inadvertently says something else, or he is almost indifferent as to whether his words mean anything or not. This mixture of vagueness and sheer incompetence is the most marked characteristic of modern English prose.'

George Orwell, *Politics and the English Language*, 1946

We could so easily write better. Despite dealing daily with subjects of life, death and drama involving most of the issues closest to the hearts of all their various audiences, too many for-change organisations, particularly INGOs, describe their work in lengthy, dense reports where the reader loses the will to live half-way down page three, if not earlier. If excess, ill-structured words were not enough, they add in obstacles such as acronyms, jargon, internal speak and sheer gobbledegook. If the raw material for our stories is so good, surely the best way to save the world would be to communicate better when we describe what we do and why we're here? Teaching communication skills to campaigning fundraisers – now, there's a radical idea!

LINKS TO MORE ON THE POWER OF WORDS

https://sofii.org/article/communication-and-the-english-language
https://sofii.org/article/twelve-suggestions-and-a-bit-more-to-help-you-write-effectively
https://sofii.org/article/the-customers-always-write
https://sofii.org/article/the-last-word-how-copywriters-can-change-the-world

47 Brilliant storytelling:
celebrating the great fundraising writers

WHY I CHOSE THIS

Great storytelling is at the heart of fundraising communication because, we now know, it works far better than anything else. Better than statistics, better than sterile reporting, better than graphs and diagrams and, well, any other form of verbal or written reporting. Boring stories, unsurprisingly, are more numerous and work much less well. So, it pays to study the best, search out your own great stories and learn the art and craft of inspirational storytelling. Besides, who doesn't love a good story?

> **'Recent scientific work is putting a much finer point on just how stories change our attitudes, beliefs and behaviours... By taking blood before and after the narrative, we found that character-driven stories do consistently cause oxytocin synthesis. Further, the amount of oxytocin released by the brain predicted how much people were willing to help others; for example, donating money to a charity associated with the narrative.'**
>
> Professor Paul J Zak, 'Why Your Brain Loves Good Storytelling', *Harvard Business Review*, 28 October 2014

ORIGINS AND OBJECTIVES

If we want to raise money consistently and cost-effectively, we need to build the relationships that underpin long-term support. The more imaginative and involving our narratives, the better. So (as I used to relate, half-

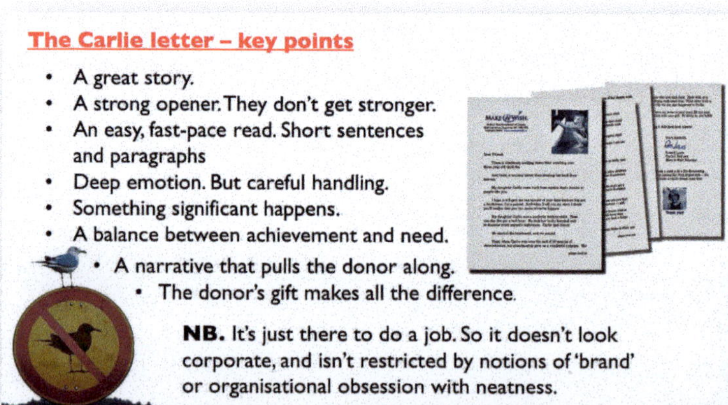

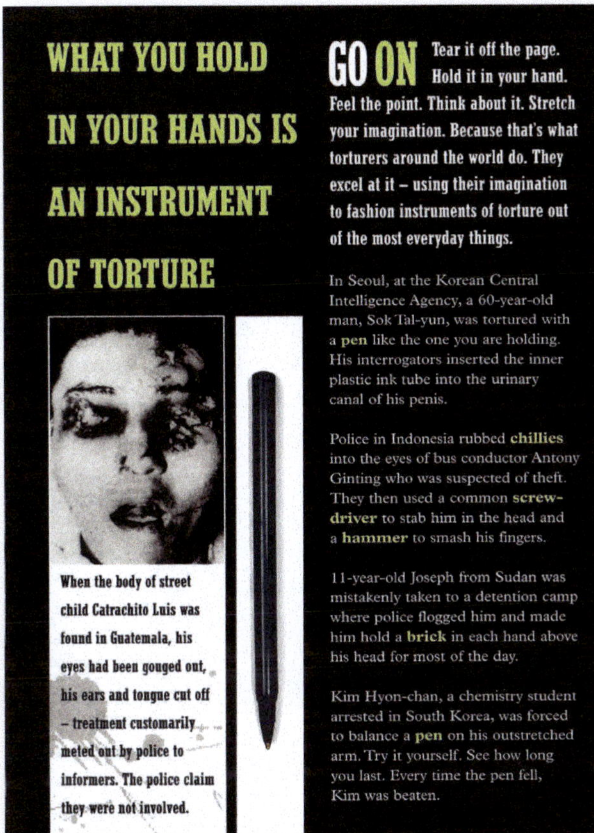

jokingly, to make a point), at major donor events we now no longer need to hide a syringe full of the hormone oxytocin behind our backs, then when the donor least expects it, step forward and squirt it up his or her nose, risking arrest in the process. We just need to learn to tell them great stories.

Scientific debate about the precise influence of oxytocin in encouraging generosity may rumble on (if you Google oxytocin you'll find a ton of learned articles, mostly positive though many inconclusive if not contradictory) but there's no doubt about the efficacy of storytelling in getting campaigning fundraising messages not just out, but through. Donors love them, particularly when focused on what their gifts achieve.

SIGNIFICANCE AND SPECIAL CHARACTERISTICS

Emotional storytelling – the truth, told well – is the key that unlocks generosity in our donors, consistently, particularly when you can put your donor him or herself into the story. Creativity in fundraising is legendary – decades ago when I used to be invited to judge the British Direct Marketing

Awards, all the 'creative' judges, selected from the most eminent in direct response advertising, always wanted to judge the fundraising category because that, they realised, was where the best creativity would be found. Not surprising really, as fundraisers have the best stories and the best of reasons for telling them well.

BACKGROUND STORY

Charities produce vast volumes of information but very little communication. Information is giving out; communication is getting through. We get through when we tell our stories well and consistently, with power, passion and professionalism that will move people to action. Yet as stated in the preceding exhibit, it remains one of the most baffling characteristics of modern fundraising, that more emphasis is not routinely put on the centrality of effective writing and storytelling skills in the modern campaigning fundraiser.

IMPACT, INFLUENCE AND OPPORTUNITIES

Over 14 years a formidable collection of fine writing for fundraising has been built up on SOFII, including the world's largest illustrated archive of case histories of fundraising direct mail, the best ever donor acquisition letter, the greatest fundraising letters of all time and much more besides.

Studying the best writers for fundraising is a sure-fire cure for any hint of writer's block, so these writers repay frequent visiting. Why their study is not actually mandatory among young fundraisers remains an open question.

LINKS TO MORE ON BRILLIANT STORYTELLING

https://sofii.org/article/sofii-stars-great-fundraising-writers
https://sofii.org/case-study/amnesty-international-the-pen-pack
https://sofii.org/article/the-a-to-z-of-writing-fundraising-appeals-a-to-f
https://sofii.org/article/how-i-wrote-it-the-make-a-wish-foundations-prospect-letter

Plus many other features in the 'How I wrote it' series.

HOW THE AGITATOR SEES IT:

http://agitator.thedonorvoice.com/what-makes-for-a-good-piece-of-fundraising-copy

48 The bad and the best: the world's worst advertisements and its most successful

WHY I CHOSE THIS

Sometimes we can learn from our mistakes, though invariably it's cheaper, easier and more satisfying to learn from the mistakes of others. Luckily for us there's a near inexhaustible supply, they're hugely instructive and they're readily available.

ORIGINS AND OBJECTIVES

Successes however tend to be a more fertile learning ground. Plagiarism is the sincerest form of flattery and the most productive too, but you always have to ensure that you add to the original rather than diminish it. Creatively, studying failures as well as successes can be instructive in terms of both what to do and what not to do.

A great way of testing fundraising competence is to run past your experienced candidate a few of both bad and good examples, then test his or her immediate reactions.

SIGNIFICANCE AND SPECIAL CHARACTERISTICS

SOFII's *Bad Ads* showcase is one of its most frequently visited corners, proving that we like few things more than revelling in the public foolishness of others. Though, while collecting stories of success is difficult enough, perhaps unsurprisingly it's harder to get people to volunteer their failures – so SOFII collects them, from those already published in the public domain. As an antidote, to show SOFII favours the good ahead of the bad, I've included here the Covenant House letter overleaf plus a link to the *Best of the Best* showcase, overleaf, where the full Covenant House letter is included.

BACKGROUND STORY

If you want people to read and respond to your ad it's unwise to reverse the type out of a dark background (particularly in the coupon – unless your readers have pens that write in white ink). Also, don't set the type too small, don't use sans serif type for body text, or over-design or try to be clever or leave out the call to action or, or... or commit a hundred other equally avoidable sins of ignorance. Yet charity advertisers do all these things, again and again, seemingly without regard. So, they should be called out, because that's good donors' money they're wasting. Perhaps the only benefit is that others can learn from their silliness.

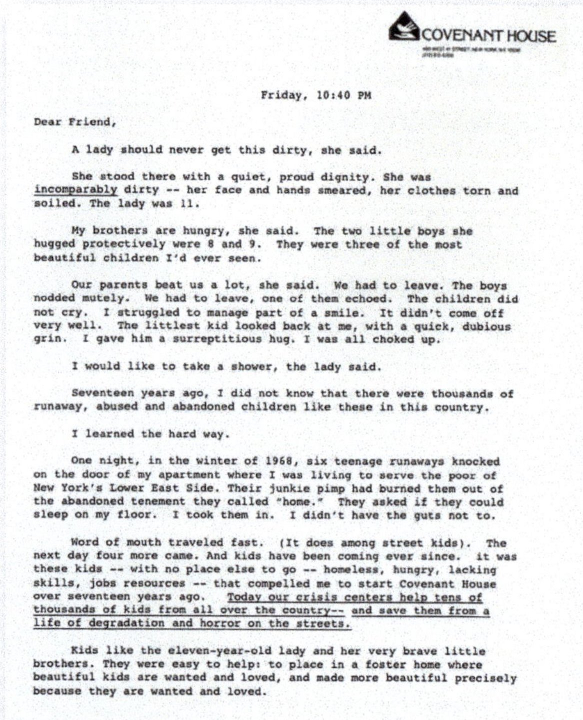

COVENANT HOUSE

Friday, 10:40 PM

Dear Friend,

A lady should never get this dirty, she said.

She stood there with a quiet, proud dignity. She was incomparably dirty -- her face and hands smeared, her clothes torn and soiled. The lady was 11.

My brothers are hungry, she said. The two little boys she hugged protectively were 8 and 9. They were three of the most beautiful children I'd ever seen.

Our parents beat us a lot, she said. We had to leave. The boys nodded mutely. We had to leave, one of them echoed. The children did not cry. I struggled to manage part of a smile. It didn't come off very well. The littlest kid looked back at me, with a quick, dubious grin. I gave him a surreptitious hug. I was all choked up.

I would like to take a shower, the lady said.

Seventeen years ago, I did not know that there were thousands of runaway, abused and abandoned children like these in this country.

I learned the hard way.

One night, in the winter of 1968, six teenage runaways knocked on the door of my apartment where I was living to serve the poor of New York's Lower East Side. Their junkie pimp had burned them out of the abandoned tenement they called "home." They asked if they could sleep on my floor. I took them in. I didn't have the guts not to.

Word of mouth traveled fast. (It does among street kids). The next day four more came. And kids have been coming ever since. It was these kids -- with no place else to go -- homeless, hungry, lacking skills, jobs resources -- that compelled me to start Covenant House over seventeen years ago. Today our crisis centers help tens of thousands of kids from all over the country-- and save them from a life of degradation and horror on the streets.

Kids like the eleven-year-old lady and her very brave little brothers. They were easy to help: to place in a foster home where beautiful kids are wanted and loved, and made more beautiful precisely because they are wanted and loved.

IMPACT, INFLUENCE AND OPPORTUNITIES

Bad ads are potentially so instructive we should start the 'Foot in Mouth Awards' to annually recognise and publicise their originators. Why not? There are already enough awards recognising excellence. The link below to the *Best of the Best* on SOFII will also take you to what is, arguably, the best ad of all time. And to the world's only fundraising beermat – unless you know of another...

LINKS TO MORE ON THE BAD AND THE BEST

https://sofii.org/case-study/greenpeace-portugal-the-unfortunate-example-of-the-reversed-out-coupon

https://sofii.org/the-fundraisers-toolbox/bad-ads-showcase

https://sofii.org/foundations-of-fundraising/best-of-the-best

https://sofii.org/article/the-most-successful-advertisement-in-the-history-of-the-world

49 Spending time with the scientists: mastering data, technology and behavioural science

WHY I CHOSE THIS

'Even after more than four decades it's still possible to learn something remarkable about our profession.' So I wrote with appropriate brio in a review of Steve MacLaughlin's game-changing book *Data Driven Nonprofits*. Shockingly, among all that I'd learned was just how ineptly, imperfectly and misguidedly modern-day fundraisers have been following fundraising's early pioneers. The justification of this conclusion from Steve comes from his analysis of how disastrously fundraisers fail to understand and invest to take advantage of the complex technologies upon which they now all depend. I'm sure none of the others cited in this section would disagree with him.

ORIGINS AND OBJECTIVES

Room for one more? Fundraisers need to know their way around data and how to manage it.

Put simply, most fundraisers don't have a joined-up strategy for implementing available technologies and latest science-based findings effectively. It's time they made sure they did. Among the many anecdotes Blackbaud's former chief scientist Chuck Longfield might regale you with, he cites one that shows how valuable such information can be. If a donor gets in touch to tell you of a change to his or her address, they are special indeed – many times more likely than the average donor to do anything that you ask of them. Why? Because for anyone to take the trouble to tell you such a seemingly mundane thing, that should tell you he or she really cares and doesn't want to lose touch. Yet priceless though they might prove, most charities don't record such interactions.

SIGNIFICANCE AND SPECIAL CHARACTERISTICS

Fundraisers' all-important relationships with their donors will have, somewhere in the background, a database as their cornerstone, though historically they'll most likely have struggled to optimise its potential, mostly because of underinvestment and general incomprehension of the possibilities it presents. Access to and control of data is much more restricted now, by state diktat. This trend will continue, for sure, as it's in the interests of donors, so fundraisers should accept and embrace the changes. Plus, the technology rockets forward, so there's no excuse for not putting time, effort and resources into mastering our use of data and applying that to our causes, to more surely save the world. Luckily, through this maze there are some exemplary guides.

> **'Harnessing the insight from data to drive decisions has the potential to transform the amount of change non-profits can make in the world...[yet] a generous estimate suggests that any form of advanced analytics is used at only three per cent of the non-profit organizations in the United States.'**
>
> Steve MacLaughlin, *Data Driven Nonprofits, 2016*

BACKGROUND STORY

It's not just data and technologies. Central to campaigning fundraising is the new field (to me at least) of behavioural science. Behavioural science is the study of human actions flowing from understanding behaviour, attitudes and motivations. It usually includes the fields of sociology, social and cultural anthropology, psychology, as well as behavioural aspects of biology, economics, geography, law, psychiatry and political science (fundraising should never be assumed to be either simple or easy). Behavioural science can inform understanding of why people give to charity and in which circumstances donations are more or less likely. So of course, a robust appreciation of it should be threaded through every campaigning fundraiser's DNA.

IMPACT, INFLUENCE AND OPPORTUNITIES

These new frontiers seem at this stage to be limitless. When it comes to heeding our sages and gurus you've just got to listen to these people, the scientists. Here are a couple of examples.

> **'There's no value in sitting on a pile of gold or a reservoir of oil that you don't have any means to access... Maybe the real killer idea for most organisations would be to make better use of their data so that they can develop more meaningful relationships with their donors.'**
>
> Chuck Longfield, former chief scientist, Blackbaud Inc, USA.

'We know that offline giving is still larger than online donations, but there is a clear shift happening. Charities should be careful not to confuse channel of engagement with the channel of transaction. The most valuable and loyal donors are engaged through multiple channels and give both online and offline. Charities need to be responsive to donor channel preferences.'

Steve MacLaughlin, *Data Driven Nonprofits, 2016*

There's not enough space in a dozen of these books to list the benefits of getting right the science that underpins campaigning fundraising. Following the links is a good place to start. Hat-tips too to professors Adrian Sargeant and Jen Shang and their colleagues, and to Bernard Ross, plus to Kevin Schulman, Dr Kiki Koutmeridou and colleagues at DonorVoice. These are among the masters worth listening to (see also exhibit 18), for they're leading the change our sector needs to see. Sargeant and Shang's Institute of Sustainable Philanthropy offers a (superb, I'm reliably informed) eight-week certificate course on philanthropic psychology backed by a mountain of research and results. Not knowing where to look becomes an ever less credible excuse.

LINKS TO MORE FROM THE FUNDRAISING SCIENTISTS

https://sofii.org/article/the-great-donor-exodus-and-what-to-do-about-it-a-three-part-series-from-jay-love

https://sofii.org/article/data-is-gold.-but-only-if-you-can-get-to-its-real-value

https://sofii.org/article/how-we-deal-with-data-why-it-matters-and-why-weve-really-got-to-get-this-right-right-now

https://sofii.org/article/the-use-and-misuse-of-emotion

https://sofii.org/article/ask-a-behavioural-scientist-pt-1

HOW THE AGITATOR SEES IT:

http://agitator.thedonorvoice.com/the-behavioral-science-of-fundraising-metrics

50 Liberating leadership: the new responsibilities of trustee boards and senior management

WHY I CHOSE THIS

It should go without saying that the senior leadership teams in each individual charity are the key players who should be driving the necessary changes in fundraising practices – the trustees and senior management teams (SMTs). I've worked with hundreds of charity boards and SMTs and while many are great, sadly, in my experience, charity leadership far too often falls short in this responsibility, largely because they simply don't sufficiently understand how fundraising works and fail to invest adequately in key aspects of it. Despite multiple examples of individual excellence there's so much that needs to change in our sector's approach to leadership and trustee training, particularly to strengthen and preserve the 'parallel boards' structure that's such a potential strength of our sector, yet so often fails to work well in practice.

ORIGINS AND OBJECTIVES

Failure to understand the distinction between the board's role of governance and oversight and the management team's role as executive managers remains a cause of much grief in the charity sector. Implementing a donor experience-based strategy and crafting an appropriate promise to all donors are the responsibilities of the director of

View from the top: are bad boards still fundraisers' biggest bugbear? If so, that needs to change.

fundraising, but to have any chance they have to be backed by the CEO and SMT colleagues and encouraged and supported by all trustees.

SIGNIFICANCE AND SPECIAL CHARACTERISTICS

It would make such a difference to the health and vitality of giving if trustee boards could develop a sound understanding of donor-based fundraising and how fundraising departments should be structured and equipped for the new era of responsible fundraising. It's generally appreciated that leadership is the art of creating greatness in other people but the context for this in fundraising departments is too seldom understood. The beginnings of a blueprint for this already exists in report 15 of the Commission on the Donor Experience, *The role of trustee boards and senior managers*, linked below, and the other CDE summaries and reports. These now need to be picked up, extended and implemented across the for-change sector.

BACKGROUND STORY

Collectively, we're all dedicated to achieving change: charity, fundraiser, donor, volunteer, community, government, beneficiaries. The best outcomes are the ones where we all come together to create the tipping point. The CDE report above concludes that, 'if fundraising is going to continue to thrive, UK charities must reframe their thinking to become truly donor- and community centred' (see also the 10 keys to community-centric fundraising, page 189). There's a long way to go to achieve this. It's worth repeating that too often boards are seen as, and actually are, an obstacle to get around rather than a support that will add value and aid decision-making. And that the most common concern voiced at fundraising conferences is, 'that's a great idea but I'll never get it past our trustees'.

SOFII trustee Richard Turner suggests a simple explanation for why trustees and fundraising often don't gel. When charities were first formed and set up to be governed by trustees it was usually in response to large gifts bequeathed by some rich benefactor. Hence the need for a group of people to oversee the use of funds in trust. And so the emphasis historically was on looking after funds, not raising them. Hence all the statutory needs of trustees are to do with how money is spent and not how funds can be invested so more can be done to achieve the mission. This, quite simply, has to change and boards have to actively learn how to play their proper leadership role so that they can bring to reality the new era of responsible fundraising.

A further shortcoming is that too often it's the board that appoints senior leadership, rather than the other way round. Boards may have the responsibility to appoint or de-appoint the CEO (not her or his SMT – that's the job of the CEO), yet things invariably work better when the charity's executive leadership at least plays a part in selecting and developing the board it needs, even if the actual appointment/de-appointment decisions remain firmly the province of the trustees.

IMPACT, INFLUENCE AND OPPORTUNITIES

Changing the culture of fundraising has to be led by trustee boards working hand in glove with senior management teams. Read Simone Joyaux on better boards and how to fire your board, on SOFII – no one covers the subject better (though there are many others well worth reading). One major priority for leadership should be the training and equipping of campaigning fundraisers to be an effective client. What an impact that would have on how well senior executives spend their charity's money.

Another similar impact could come from inculcating best thinking and practice across all staff functions, along with instilling a sound grasp of the essential foundations of fundraising (exhibit 3). For the for-change sector this would be liberating indeed.

LINKS TO MORE ON LEADERSHIP

https://sofii.org/article/cde-project-15-summary-the-role-of-trustee-boards-and-senior-managers
https://sofii.org/article/firing-lousy-board-members
https://sofii.org/article/how-precisely-do-you-build-a-better-board-part-1
https://sofii.org/article/contradictory-signs-as-the-corona-crisis-continues
https://sofii.org/the-fundraisers-toolbox/how-to-be-an-effective-client

HOW THE AGITATOR SEES IT:

http://agitator.thedonorvoice.com/the-great-fundraising-comeback

51 Fundraising at times of crisis: delivering help quickly and effectively to where it's needed most

WHY I CHOSE THIS

I cut my teeth fundraising for aid in the wake of a disaster. Somehow back then, emergencies always seemed to happen at weekends, though that may just be an impression and anyway we had a plan that allowed for it.

ORIGINS AND OBJECTIVES

Whenever a major flood, earthquake or typhoon struck anywhere in the world, speed was always paramount. To get aid quickly to those in need we first had to raise the money to pay for everything. That meant placing the right message in the right places at a speed unthinkable in normal times.

SIGNIFICANCE AND SPECIAL CHARACTERISTICS

Whenever a substantial disaster struck anywhere in the world, I would phone my mentor Harold Sumption (see exhibit 3). Harold had refined this approach over years at Oxfam and Help the Aged. Creative content was just the essentials, presented as dramatically as possible, as if we were reporting from the front line of a war sometime around the end of the 19th century. If the scale of disaster merited it, we'd launch an appeal, so I'd scoot round to Harold's house to draft and agree copy and where to place it. We had a list of addresses and home phone numbers for ad directors in the quality newspapers, our banker media. If the disaster happened on a Saturday, we would phone our text through inside 24 hours and the ads would appear in Monday morning's newspapers. Now digital and social media fundraising are almost instantaneous in response to disasters and news plus appeals can be placed and followed in real-time, as the situation evolves. Few activities could rival this for excitement, adrenalin and intensity. Particularly when those life-saving donations flood in...

BACKGROUND STORY

Disaster advertising is a very distinct, specialised sub-genre of fundraising. My experiences described above happened before ActionAid joined the exclusive club of major UK aid organisations, the incomparable Disasters Emergency Committee (DEC). This unique coalition of 14 leading UK aid charities is perhaps the most experienced, most effective organisation raising funds for humanitarian disasters anywhere. It's the envy of the fundraising world.

IMPACT, INFLUENCE AND OPPORTUNITIES

The public, particularly donors, loves the DEC, because it's the perfect example of charities working collaboratively and effectively together for the common good. For sure they'd love any similar coalition if only more such initiatives could follow DEC's example – cancer research, climate change, Black Lives Matter, help lines, community-based initiatives… You name it, the world will benefit when fundraisers come together to give donors what they want to see – their chosen charities serving their favourite causes better by working brilliantly well, together.

Without doubt, a crisis is the best time ever to mobilise campaigning and raise really large sums cost-effectively. Despite sector-wide handwringing and predictions of plummeting fundraising performance in just about every fundraising market the Covid-19 pandemic of the early 2020s turned out to be a hugely successful opportunity for fundraising from individual regular donors, all wanting to feel good by giving from accumulated funds they were mostly unable to spend. Again, this counter-intuitive outcome is unique to this business area and remains widely under-appreciated, even within those organisations that could benefit directly from it.

LINKS TO MORE ON FUNDRAISING AT A TIME OF CRISIS

https://sofii.org/case-study/rcsb-bhopal-emergency-appeal
https://sofii.org/article/bridging-the-empathy-gap
https://sofii.org/article/peoples-generosity-during-tragic-times
https://sofii.org/article/cde-project-6-section-4-8-craig-linton-and-paul-stein-on-emotion

HOW THE AGITATOR SEES IT:

http://agitator.thedonorvoice.com/get-em-while-the-grief-is-hot-part-1

52 Fundraisers together: working and helping each other through tough times

WHY I CHOSE THIS

Continuing the theme of disaster fundraising, one characteristic of fundraisers' response to the worldwide pandemic of 2020/21 has been a flurry of instances of fundraisers helping each other. From many inspiring initiatives, lack of space requires me to select just a few goodies.

ORIGINS AND OBJECTIVES

The voluntary sector is justly proud that it's always shared resources and supported its own, even those that might be seen as in direct competition. Social media has helped this – help groups and chatrooms abound alongside free-to-access websites, podcasts and webinars. Charities embarking on a fundraising initiative new to their organisation can easily seek out help and advice from experienced people in other organisations who will give their time and expertise freely and substantially. Free resources spring up online all the time. Since the advent of the Covid-19 pandemic these have positively blossomed.

> **'[I'm] a bit astonished that fundraisers were the first people to get furloughed at this time, because I thought they were never more needed, they were absolutely essential.'**
>
> Anna Fowlie, chief executive, the Scottish Council of Voluntary Organisations

In the UK huge numbers of charity staff were furloughed in the first weeks of the government's job protection scheme. Amazingly the leadership in their organisations seemed to imagine their fundraising wouldn't suffer without the fundraisers. Or, in a crazy self-fulfilling prophecy, they assumed decline was inevitable. Suffer and decline it did, for many, of course. The dramatic exceptions to this, unsurprisingly, were those organisations that empowered their fundraisers to reach out and show concern and support for their regular donors, many of whom had few of their usual activities to spend their money on, yet at such a time they really wanted to do something practical to help. As has been extensively documented, those organisations prospered, recording responses 'better than Christmas' at the pandemic's height.

SIGNIFICANCE AND SPECIAL CHARACTERISTICS

Furloughed Fundraisers Chat (FFC) in the UK offered a space for fundraisers released by their employers to feel connected to fundraising during the global pandemic, providing self-help, encouraging resilience, supporting networking and learning. While this was happening, Italy's top consultants got together to offer free help to fundraisers in their country's health sector. And New Zealand's professional body, the Fundraising Institute of New Zealand (FINZ), launched an emergency appeal among fundraisers around the world to stave off looming insolvency caused by the sudden collapse of training events. For many people the present had become scarily precarious and the future frighteningly uncertain. So, it's to the credit of our sector that at such times, fundraisers rally to help each other.

BACKGROUND STORY

Very many charities were badly hit during this time of huge adversity and others assumed they would be. So, when the UK government announced it would pay charities up to 80 per cent of an employee's wages to 'furlough' their staff (ie pay them to sit at home) 160,000 charity staff were furloughed in the first six weeks of the scheme, including many fundraisers. Given that these organisations were anticipating dramatic falls in their incomes, this was curious, perhaps the opposite of what logic might suggest they should be doing – surely if income is falling you need your fundraisers more than ever? The Government's scheme decreed that furloughed employees can't do fundraising for their own cause but can raise money for someone else's, so FFC created space for charities to find fantastic fundraisers eager to do something really useful during their time on furlough.

In a variety of ways fundraisers have offered their specialist expertise to help others struggling to survive the pandemic. The 40 Italian consultants

who came together to advise and support components of the Italian health service are a superb example of this. When the financial impact of the pandemic hit, spontaneous fundraising initiatives took root all across Italy, but most were lacking in know-how and experience of running fundraising campaigns. Enter the specially created Task Force, whose members could be drafted in to help as required. And when events, training and conferences cancelled because of the pandemic threatened the financial viability and continued existence of New Zealand's professional body for fundraisers, SOFII was able to document a revolutionary new kind of fundraising campaign, fundraisers chipping in to help each other.

IMPACT, INFLUENCE AND OPPORTUNITIES

Sticking together, all pulling as one, very often turns adversity to advantage. Despite the current challenges, these initiatives show that campaigning fundraisers are well on the way to getting right just what the new era of responsible fundraising will need.

When times get tough, prudent investment in what works might prove better than cost-cutting. There's much more to be gained by pulling together, supporting each other and showing our caring side, to see everyone's alright – particularly our colleagues and donors. At such a time, enterprising campaigning fundraisers can and will show a lead to the world.

Unquestionably, the opportunities are there now for further cooperation by campaigning fundraisers, with the clear agenda of realising their full potential to be the change that their supporters and their societies all want to see.

LINKS TO MORE ON FUNDRAISERS WORKING TOGETHER

https://sofii.org/case-study/italys-fundraising-taskforce-for-hospitals
https://sofii.org/case-study/furloughed-fundraisers-chat-ffc
https://sofii.org/article/save-finz-a-fundraiser-to-fundraiser-f2f-appeal

HOW THE AGITATOR SEES IT:

http://agitator.thedonorvoice.com/the-naughty-the-nice-the-unappreciated

CONCLUSION

The dream: building a better future for campaigning fundraisers, their causes and their donors

'The stand-out takeaway from this report is the positivity surrounding fundraisers, confirming their ability to directly impact causes and their undeniable value to the non-profits they serve. Fundraisers are vital to the sector and will continue to play a significant role in its future. They are the superstars who keep the industry thriving, raising millions for non-profits every year. We believe fundraisers should be celebrated, and the findings of our report are undeniable proof of this.'

Lianne McGrory, managing director, Blackbaud Europe,
from *The Status of UK Fundraising 2018 Benchmark Report*

THE DREAM: BUILDING A BETTER FUTURE

It seems to me remarkable that Lianne McGrory's assurance needs to be given. But it does, constantly, because so few people – fundraisers themselves included – are familiar with all the great things fundraisers do and the tremendous good they make possible. Even fewer have any deep understanding of their illustrious, instructive past and the promise and potential of their future. It's to be hoped this book will help change that, because elevating and celebrating for-change sector superstars is long overdue.

If you don't know how you've got here it's unlikely you'll know where here is or where you could get to from here if you really try. Of course we can't change the past, but we can learn from it, to equip ourselves more effectively to change the future. Though it has to be asked, have we got what it takes to promptly change that future? Have we got what it takes to learn from even our recent past?

PREPARING FOR THE NEW ERA

In this (one has to assume) soon to be post-pandemic world, predicting the future (something I used to get to do every five years or so, see my blogs, linked below) seems like a mug's game. So, I'm not going to try. The best I can do instead is to set out here what could be possible, what I believe we should be doing to prepare for and bring about the new era of responsible fundraising that the 52 exhibits featured here build up to, together. So, this final section tries to define what campaigning fundraisers might aspire to, in terms of our role in society, the current parlous state of our political and social leadership and some key things we've learned from our sector's rich, illustrious past and particularly from everything that's been going so badly wrong recently.

There's much that's worrying, even terrifying, when we look at today's deep global trends. Among the most frightening of these is what US President Barack Obama has termed 'truth decay', a phenomenon so deeply rooted in our political leadership that it may be impossible to eradicate.

> **'Brace yourself, the flood of lies in this election is about to become a torrent... Our political honour code is breaking down. This post-truth election is a taster of what could be to come...taking us further into the abyss.'**
>
> *The Observer*, UK, 8 December 2019

There is no sanction now, when politicians lie openly to their publics. They can get away with it, even prosper by it. This to some seems potentially copyable and to have many benefits. We must oppose that.

For the charity sector, dependent as it is on the trust, confidence and unshakeable belief of donors, any further slide towards truth decay could be terminal. Yet some signs of hope and opportunity can perhaps be found for campaigning fundraisers. Though in our populace as a whole, optimism about the future seems to have fallen through the floor, for sure there are reasons to be cheerful too. One of the most encouraging of

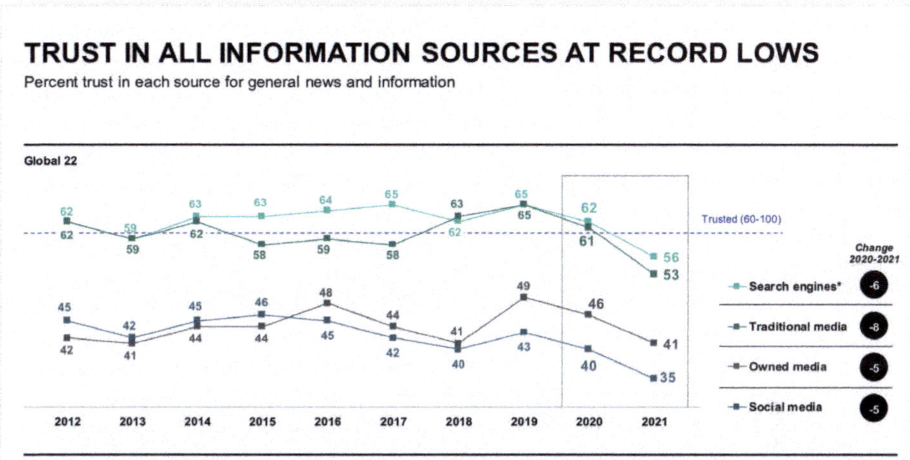

From 2021 Edelman Trust Barometer

these is the emerging opportunity for voluntary/ for-change/ not-for-profit organisations[1] to lead a social revolution in changing their culture and personalities so they can better provide their multiple benefits and care for society's weaker, more vulnerable members.

But the environment within which the for-change sector operates is likely to get more rather than less hostile. Despite widespread efforts at fiscal stimulus throughout the pandemic, forecasters generally predict a deep and lasting post Covid-19 global recession. This comes at a particularly dangerous time for our entire species and our voluntary sector organisations evidently are not immune from this. Worryingly, the risk of further, perhaps even worse viral outbreaks hasn't reduced, with all that implies. Yet global pandemics and economic collapses apart, there are other, arguably bigger threats. Climate catastrophe is looming large with apocalyptic implications for both our wellbeing and our wallets. Species

1 Delete as appropriate – our sector should, as a matter of priority, agree on a positive name that we can all unite behind. I'd opt for the for-change sector. That sounds positive and optimistic, to me.

extinctions, extreme weather, rising temperatures and sea levels, health risks, droughts, floods. Nothing about climate change looks good. At risk is the very continuance of our species itself.

Add to this evidence that many among our publics are losing their appetite for authority, their tolerance for alternative views and are increasingly self-centred, negative, shallow and easily bored. People now give no automatic respect to their political leaders, who clearly fail them regularly, visibly and with seeming impunity.

WE DEPEND ON PUBLIC TRUST AND CONFIDENCE

Stemming from this leadership vacuum is a growing absence of trust and confidence in the probity and moral standards of not just politicians and business leaders but of many figures in public life. The for-change sector has been largely insulated so far, principally because of the fine intentions of our donors, who whatever the shortcomings of those who set out to exploit their giving, won't let the causes they support suffer, come what may. Well, up to a point they won't. As we learned in 2015, we must not push that point.

We need to inspire and entice more donors. As society places increasing calls upon our organisations, they in turn are ever more dependent on supporters who will provide the money and the volunteers upon which for-change organisations so depend. So we need to find more ways to inspire more people to see that it's in their direct personal interests to actively support the causes that campaigning fundraisers work for and care so passionately about. Commercial companies often with questionable motives and self-interest are increasingly wearing the clothes of campaigning for-change organisations. People care more and more about the policies and practices of the companies they are buying from. At the very least, these trends should keep us on our toes.

It's possible to see all this as hope for a new dawn. It's beyond my capacity or remit to present here a detailed, rigorous catalogue of today's social ills, so I won't attempt it. But I do believe the decline in standards and values elsewhere gives the for-change sector a massive opportunity. Amongst all other business areas, our sector should be a paragon of justice, decency, fairness, equality, honesty, integrity, diversity and morality. Across society, throughout this pandemic, we have seen multiple small acts of care, consideration and kindness. It's at the macro level of politics and at the extreme right and left hand ends of the spectrum that things have gone terribly wrong.

Embracing the new dawn is not just for our self-preservation, it's also a massive opportunity for growth. Our sector has a chance now to emerge as the standard-bearer for doing good and doing what's right. Which will pay off big time as our constituencies will respond generously. We can be society's conscience, a beacon of rightness, openness, transparency and accountability in public life. It's vastly in our sector's interests to be so, because donors will love it, those same donors who fund everything we do. We risk losing many of those donors if we don't. We may win back some already lost if we do.

Our sector isn't quite there, of course, at least not yet, not nearly. But it could be. The vacuum outlined needs to be filled. Why not by us? Countering a few of these negative global trends is within our power, provided we can prioritise doing the right thing ahead of raising the most money now. If we do that, ultimately it will enable us to raise lots more money overall, in the long term.

Campaigning fundraisers could take a lead and encourage culture change

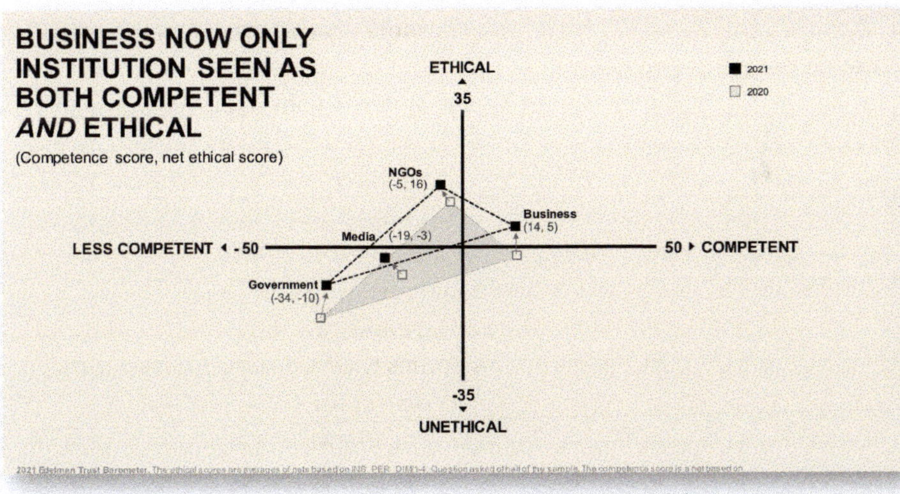

From 2021 Edelman Trust Barometer

in several specific areas. Apart from leading all other businesses in fairness, morality, integrity, equity, diversity and justice we could define a culture of prudent risk-taking and of standing up consistently for high beliefs and standards, for enterprise, creativity and innovation. But instead, charities tend to be risk averse and to avoid conflict even when it's called for. There are of course glorious exceptions to that sweeping statement.

Emotional intelligence and empathy also both seem in short supply, so we could train our colleagues in these high-value skills. We could elevate leadership in all our organisations and ensure the standards we demand of our sector leaders are the clearest, most achievable and most inspirational to be found anywhere. We could reshape our culture in key areas and use the changes to encourage coming generations, the young people who through their work want to make a difference and change the world, so they'll choose us as the best available route.

As always, people desperately want something to believe in – that market is infinite – but right now our political leaders have comprehensively shown themselves to be less and less capable of delivering that. So, the people need to look elsewhere for something to believe in. Why not to the for-change sector, if it can change, restructure and step up to the mark?

And change it must. In the UK for far too long the voluntary sector, led predominantly by stuffy, conservative, middle class, generally elderly white men, has been apprehensive of risk, under-investing and stuck in a decline of its own making. Yet as a business sector, major employer and as a significant part of our society it's important, substantial, vital and – though it can do better, – for the most part, it's thriving, even through a pandemic. We have to commit to making this change now.

Why not? Changing the world is indeed the only fit work for a grown man or woman. Everyone should be a part of it. We can ensure all have that chance.

I don't expect everyone to agree. Why should they? They never have, so far. But many will. They are the changemakers.

GIVING CAN BE MUCH MORE ATTRACTIVE AND WIDESPREAD

To progress we need to make giving much more attractive and rewarding to many more people. And we can. The shifting economic, social and political landscapes tell us it won't be easy. But it will be very positive and satisfying, not just for our for-change sector organisations but also for individual donors and for our society as a whole. And for campaigning fundraisers too.

To fit this book's key lessons into a manageable 52 exhibits and 199 web links, inevitably I've had to leave out many important aspects of the full fundraising picture, purely on grounds of lack of available space. So, I've decided not to say anything substantial here about charity regulation, volunteering, trading, Just Giving and similar initiatives, Giving Tuesday (which is getting impressive traction around the world), the fast-developing area of digital fundraising, government underfunding, activist campaigning and a range of other significant issues. It's not that I don't think these areas important, merely that I had to leave many things out and as these are generally outside of my expertise, they were obvious candidates for exclusion. I'm emphasising what follows as particularly important, because it's here that I can see change is coming. And it's essential, I believe, that campaigning fundraisers themselves structure and direct that change.

THE PRINCIPLES OF COMMUNITY-CENTRIC FUNDRAISING

According to their website, Community-Centric Fundraising is a movement to evolve how fundraising is done in the non-profit sector. Its goal is to support fundraisers and other non-profit professionals to re-examine every fundraising philosophy and practice they have been taught, engage in vigorous ongoing conversations and explore doing fundraising in ways that reduce harm and further social justice.

I admire this initiative and I'm encouraged to see serious consideration of fundraising under a justice and racial equity lens. That doesn't mean I agree with everything the community-centric fundraising people are setting out, but I like their principles and feel if they follow those, they won't go far wrong.

> **'These 10 Principles are how we aspire to transform fundraising and philanthropy, so that they are co-grounded in racial and economic justice... Consider these 10 Principles a starting point.'**
> From the Community-Centric Fundraising website

1. Fundraising must be grounded in race, equity, and social justice.
2. Individual organizational missions are not as important as the collective community.
3. Non-profits are generous with and mutually supportive of one another.
4. All who engage in strengthening the community are equally valued, whether volunteer, staff, donor, or board member.
5. Time is valued equally as money.
6. We treat donors as partners, and this means that we are transparent, assume the best intentions, and occasionally have difficult conversations.
7. We foster a sense of belonging, not othering.
8. We promote the understanding that everyone (donors, staff, funders,

board members, volunteers) personally benefits from engaging in the work of social justice – it's not just charity and compassion.
9 We see the work of social justice as holistic and transformative, not transactional.
10 We recognize that healing and liberation requires a commitment to economic justice.

A pretty good start, if you ask me. Add these to the lessons of history plus all we've learned from fundraising's recent mistakes and past successes, combine it with the accumulated wisdom of the inspirational sages, add in a campaigning vision, zeal, passion, courage, creativity, integrity and clarity and the new era of responsible fundraising should fall neatly into place.

ACTIVELY SETTING AN EXAMPLE

But it won't without the right leadership. The donor-based approach and delivering a consistently great supporter experience has to be insisted upon until it becomes part of each fundraiser's DNA. Trustees and senior leadership need to set an example and show the way. It's a bit like being a good waiter in a top-class hotel – no hotel manager or owner would dream of allowing anyone to serve a customer unless they'd first served their time in structured preparation for the task. That means they'd have to have had proper training, show the right attitude and aptitudes, demonstrate commitment to great service and have survived appropriate oversight through the early stages of their career. Why should charities treat their donors less well?

Obviously, we should never stop learning. While preparing this book I've been privileged to read the draft manuscript for Lisa Sargent's new book, *Thankology: a fundraiser's guide to keeping your donors longer, and giving stronger, through gratitude.* A few years back I might have skipped over a title like this, thinking it held little for me. Well, I'd have missed a lot. Reading this massively important work has shown me that helping donors everywhere to realise that they are seen, appreciated and valued is a crucial, even central component of effective fundraising, one that should be a priority for all of us. This major component of relationship fundraising has been undervalued for years. The impact on fundraising results of changing that will, I'm certain, be colossal.

Charity marketing and communications will change in the next few years I'm sure, with much more emphasis on conversation and less on persuasion, more on storytelling and engagement rather than targeting and selling, simply because great human stories unfailingly work best for us, as they build understanding, love and compassion in whoever's prepared to listen. I've yet to meet a donor who wants to be marketed at by his or her favourite causes, so while making full use of the best of marketing methodologies I hope campaigning fundraisers will drop the word marketing from their organisational descriptions and not use it when they refer to how and why they communicate with donors. They might also consider jettisoning (or at least being more careful with) unedifying, donor-unfriendly terms such as targeting, segmenting, upgrading, acquiring, lapsing, reactivating and any other descriptors that indicate we see our supporters as objects or ATMs rather than as real people. We can do better.

MISSING A TRICK – GIVING IS GOOD FOR ALL OF US

The Charities Trust's slogan proclaims, 'Giving feels good'. This is no idle boast. Our sector's famous 'warm glow' is massively powerful and felt universally. But warm glows are far from all our sector has to offer. There's such a lot we can give our donors, in return for their sustained support.

According to Dr Tara Swart, neuroscientist and senior lecturer at Massachusetts Institute of Technology, the things we most want from life – health, happiness, wealth, love – are governed by our ability to think, feel and act; in other words, by our brain. The brain's workings are something Dr Swart knows rather a lot about. In a series of short films commissioned by Barclays Private Bank Dr Swart responded to the question 'How does giving make you feel good?' by pointing out that, 'Research from neuroscience shows incredible benefits from giving, on our resilience levels, immune system and leads to better health in later life. Giving literally boosts the brain, helps reduce stress and boosts brain performance. In a world where we work so hard to be smarter, stronger and more successful we are missing a trick by not viewing mindful giving as a core piece of the puzzle.'

Wow! That's huge. And she's so right! For sure we are. Missing several tricks, I'd venture.

> **'Success, like happiness, cannot be pursued. It must ensue, and it only does so as the unintended side-effect of one's dedication to a cause greater than oneself.'**
>
> Viktor E Frankl, *Man's Search for Meaning*, 1946

Such findings are not new. In an article on *The Huffington Post* site in July 2016 entitled 'Seven science-backed reasons why giving is good for your health', journalist Amanda Chan outlined the reasons as

- It will reduce stress.
- You'll be happier.
- It'll lead to more success.
- You'll live longer.
- Your marriage will be stronger.
- You'll be mentally more healthy.
- You'll want to do more of it, so will keep getting healthier.

Blimey! If you give, your marriage will be stronger. Imagine the power in that message alone. Why do we need a bank and a news and opinions website to tell us such things? We should have been singing this proudly from the rooftops, from long ago, for ages.

This really is staggeringly important. We know donors delight in giving but they often do so in spite of rather than because of fundraisers. They give till it hurts more than they give because it's good for them. If we can elevate the role of campaigning fundraisers, foster great supporter experiences and spread the heart-warming news that giving is actually good for you as well as hugely rewarding and fulfilling, fundraising results should soon start going through the roof. It's about time. Campaigning fundraisers have been hiding their lights for way too long. It's time to change this, now.

So let's remind ourselves, what's so great about fundraising? Here's what I think:

- When you give thousands, maybe hundreds of thousands of people a great cause, something they can believe in, that's tangible, clear and engaging, that they are sure *is really worth supporting*...
- ...plus, if from the start you also give them a consistently great supporter experience, so they'll *want to stay* with you and enjoy supporting you...
- ...so then, in return, *they will give your charity* a robust, dependable and secure financial future, so you can deliver the great work your organisation does, consistently.

That's what's so great about fundraising. It works. We know it works. We have ample evidence to demonstrate it.

Truly heart-warming, inspirational, great stuff! Surely, one of the world's best stories. As I've said before and often, campaigning fundraisers have the best stories in the world and the best of reasons for telling them. Why, then, we have to wonder, is what campaigning fundraisers do not much more popular with our publics? Of course we need to change that.

The provenance of things that circulate on the internet is doubtful, their quality and accuracy suspect, their depth often shallow and the points they make subject to challenge. One that came my way recently was called *The Balance Sheet of Life*. Many of its claims may indeed be suspect but more than a few struck me as self-evidently true. What really shook me was that more than half of the list made claims that relate directly to the output of campaigning fundraisers.

Here are a few:

- The greatest joy...Giving.
- The most satisfying work...Helping others.
- The ugliest personality trait...Selfishness.
- The most effective sleeping pill...Peace of mind.
- The most powerful force in life...Love.
- The worst thing to be without...Hope.
- The two most power-filled words...I can.
- The greatest asset...Faith.
- The most beautiful attire...Smile!
- The most prized possession...Integrity.
- The most contagious spirit...Enthusiasm.

How twee, I hear you say. Yet all of these are essential components of a donor-based approach to the business of raising money. *The balance sheet of life* goes on to say, life ends when you stop dreaming, hope ends when you stop believing, love ends when you stop caring. Schmaltzy, sure, of course they are. But are these not also the core of campaigning fundraising, giving people the chance to make a difference, changing the world for the better? Maybe we have to embrace the twee, to de-twee it and make it mainstream. Our compassionate humanity is our sector's ultimate competitive edge. The best things in life are not things, and our society needs constant reminding of that. At the end of our lives, all we have to leave is our love. That sounds like a charitable legacy, to me.

So, as this book nears its end, here are ten things all fundraisers could do now, to make fundraising better:

* Be proud to be a campaigning fundraiser.
* Giving is good for you. It's provable. Spread this and get it on the national agenda.
* Advocate and agitate for morality, diversity, justice, fairness, safety and integrity throughout your organisation. Spread understanding of the achievements and benefits that this brings.
* Focus on delivering great supporter experiences. Invest in this. Get leadership buy-in.
* Promise publicly that you'll deliver a great experience for your donors and other supporters. Then show them how.
* Ensure you and your colleagues are sensibly and regularly immersed in the fundamental foundations of fundraising and its rich, informative, rewarding history.
* Tell the truth very well. You are in the inspiration business. Be bold, authentically you.
* Give at least as much as you get. Consistently.
* Treat your fundraisers very well. Equip them superbly for their refreshed role – guardians of the new era of responsible fundraising.
* Always go a bit further and give a bit extra. Remember fundraising is a profit centre, whereas services, public policy, HR, finance and other areas are cost centres.
* Communicate great feelings and add meaning to life.

OK it's eleven things. As I said, campaigning fundraisers always need to go further.

Technology will surely assist campaigning fundraisers as they seek ever better means of bringing donors and beneficiaries much closer together. Fundraising departments, organisational structures and leadership role models will change substantially. While I suspect the core of what matters most for campaigning fundraisers will fundamentally not change, I expect to be proven wrong on at least a few of my predictions before too long.

Whatever the future for fundraising brings I'm more confident now than at any time in the past 43 years that it's in good hands. So, I wish you, dear reader, the very best of luck, plus much added wisdom, foresight and the best possible grounding to point you in the right direction. I hope this book, with its 52 exhibits and 199 web links, will have helped with that. And will help you and the people you help, into the future.

LINKS

http://www.kenburnett.com/Blog55Fundraisingandtheruleoflaw.html
https://communitycentricfundraising.org/ccf-movement/

About SOFII

Telling history through things is what museums are for. So said Dr Neil MacGregor in the opening line of his book *A History of the World in 100 Objects*. SOFII – the Showcase of Fundraising Innovation and Inspiration – started life as a museum of all things to do with fundraising down the ages, but quickly grew to be something much more – a collection of collections, of course, but also a catalyst, an inspirer, a pollinator, a challenger, a history of campaigning fundraising and a platform for radical new ideas and valuable insights, plus a vehicle for promoting campaigning fundraising worldwide through the iconic talent showcase and seminar format that's known as IWITOT – *I Wish I'd Thought Of That*. (Hat-tip to all the talented, creative people who have made IWITOT such a celebration of self-selected brilliance for our sector.)

SOFII IS DEDICATED TO:

* preserving fundraising's colourful, instructive history
* spreading ideas that change the world
* celebrating inspiration and creativity
* creating an indispensable fundraiser's toolbox.
* encouraging for-change sector workers to value and celebrate their role in helping others to make a difference.

It does all this via the provision of a free, online, easily accessible archive of fundraising case studies and articles and running events to disseminate great fundraising ideas and best practice.

So SOFII is more than a museum. Museums, by definition, exist by presenting then hopefully illuminating and explaining the work of others. Over the years, museums have often let themselves down by expropriating their exhibits, obtaining and clinging onto them without appropriate permissions. For this book we've mainly relied on content which is already in the public domain, mostly content on public display on the SOFII website that has often been there for several years. As campaign materials generally have been sent out uninvited to members of the public it's deemed that they've thereby entered the public arena, so can be displayed and critiqued as SOFII sees fit. Nevertheless, SOFII invariably seeks permission from a work's creators before exhibiting its case history on the site. In some instances, when something in the public domain deserves to be added but where obtaining permission isn't practical – for example, in SOFII's *Bad Ads* showcase – it may be added anyway without permission on the understanding that, if anyone objects and a fair case for its removal can be made, SOFII can take it down.

In the spirit of the museum, I make absolutely no apology for quoting frequently and concisely from the writing and findings of others as I assemble my case for effective campaigning fundraising and how to do it right. Indeed, I've actively sought out quotable quotes so that you might have access to the best of thinking, rather than merely mine.

If gaining specific permission has not been possible, I've limited this to short extracts such as would be covered by 'fair use' and have acknowledged provenance wherever I can. Any errors or omissions of course are purely mine.

It's the entire purpose of SOFII and its thousands of case histories, ideas and articles to encourage respectful plagiarism to avoid the inconvenience, cost and time lost in reinventing the wheel. In encouraging responsible, creative copying, SOFII's policy has been to acknowledge its sources properly and always seek permission whenever practical, whether covered by copyright or not. SOFII never seeks to pass off anything borrowed as its own, instead it celebrates and promotes experts and innovators, so that the best of what's around can be shared as widely as possible, for free.

TO SIGN UP FOR SOFII'S FREE WEEKLY UPDATES PLEASE EMAIL carolina@sofii.org

https://sofii.org
https://sofii.org/article/why-should-god-have-all-the-best-ideas
https://sofii.org/article/everything-iwitot

PLEASE, DONATE TO SOFII. THANK YOU!

The SOFII Foundation is a charity registered in the UK no. 1124743 and a company limited by guarantee, company registered no. 06530274. SOFII needs your support – please donate via the link below to support SOFII today, or email joanna@sofii.org. You can shape the future of fundraising by giving your fellow fundraisers the courage and the opportunity to innovate. Your gift means you'll be helping campaigning fundraisers learn from past lessons, understand the foundations of great fundraising, build on the shoulders of the pioneers that came before them and share their successes back to SOFII so they can inspire the next generation.

Thank you for building the new era of responsible campaigning fundraising.

https://sofii.org/donate

About *The Agitator*

For the past 15 years *The Agitator* (www.agitator.thedonorvoice.com) has provided a free online service offering analysis of trends in fundraising along with practical tips – all delivered with a bit of an edge.

The founding aim – a mission that continues through to today – is to challenge complacency and conventional wisdom while applying behavioral science in practical ways for practising fundraisers through research and pilot projects conducted by its partner, DonorVoice (www.thedonorvoice.com).

These insights are provided through:

- ✶ Thrice weekly posts on a variety of topics of practical concern
- ✶ Webinars and symposia featuring DonorVoice experts and nonprofit leaders
- ✶ White papers detailing behavioral science research, results of pilot projects and test results.

The content and editorial priorities of *The Agitator* are guided by the belief that fundraising – especially direct response fundraising whether mail, digital, text or social media – will enjoy a spectacular future. Far brighter than most predict. The only truly worrisome threats to our craft are complacency and conventional wisdom. Both jeopardise the best possible performance at a time when nonprofits will be required to perform far more and far better than they have in the past.

Fundraising is a craft that, in *The Agitator*'s view, has grown too self-satisfied. Even for the inexperienced or just plain stupid, there is rapid advancement and substantial financial reward. Why? Because the number of available vacancies for 'fundraising' positions far outstrips the available talent.

Even more worrisome in this era of rapid change is the unwillingness on the part of far too many fundraisers, CEOs and Boards to innovate, to take risks and to break new ground.

Fortunately – as the work of SOFII and this book itself so clearly demonstrate – there is a wealth of new talent, technologies and techniques bursting onto the scene. These are the best antidotes to complacency and conventional wisdom.

There's no better way to shine the spotlight on the trends, talent, techniques and technologies that will make us all perform better tomorrow than we do today. After all, the stakes for the causes and organizations we serve are simply too high to accept anything less.

You can sign up for *free Agitator* issues delivered to your e-mail box by going to www.agitator.thedonorvoice.com

About the author

Ken Burnett is an internationally recognised author, consultant and inspirational speaker on fundraising, marketing and communications for non-profit organisations worldwide. He was UK director and director of fundraising and communications for ActionAid from 1977 to 1982, when he founded the influential Burnett Associates agency group, the first marketing and communications agency in Europe to specialise in working with campaigning for-change organisations. Ken is author of several seminal books including *Relationship Fundraising*, *Friends for Life*, *The Zen of Fundraising*, *Tiny Essentials of an Effective Volunteer Board* and *Storytelling can change the world*. Ken has served on quite a few trustee boards for charities large and small – from 1998 to 2003 Ken was chairman of trustees of ActionAid International, from 2012 to 2018 he was also an independent trustee of the UK Disasters Emergency Committee, with specific responsibility for fundraising. He is a former vice chair of the UK's Institute of Fundraising, is co-founder and a trustee of SOFII, the Showcase of Fundraising Innovation and Inspiration and a trustee of the World Land Trust. In 2016 Ken Burnett co-founded the Commission on the Donor Experience, with Giles Pegram CBE. When not in lockdown, travelling or giving seminars Ken spends his time between London and rural Suffolk, where he's discovered a new love for writing, directing and acting in amateur village plays.

Acknowledgements

Of all my books, plays and articles, this is the first I've taken to print without my late wife Marie's guiding hand, wise advice and caring editorial eye. As a result, the process has been much more difficult and the outcome is probably inferior in many respects. But her influence is in each of these pages, all the same. I would be remiss not to acknowledge also the help and guidance of very many others, only a few of whom I can mention here.

Joanna Culling, Carolina Herrera and Joe Burnett continue to keep SOFII together and functioning effectively, able successors to Natalie Scott and Sue Kershaw. Though, none of them is full-time and how they produce all they do is still, largely, a mystery to me. Credit for the brilliant concept that is IWITOT – I Wish I'd Thought Of That – should go to James Briggs and Tim Longfoot of Open Creates, with thanks for the fine lunch where the concept was evolved back in 2011. What more can I say, except, I wish I'd thought of I Wish I'd Thought Of That.

John Martin and Gabrielle Zagnojute from Directory of Social Change first gave me the idea for this book, or something similar, and have encouraged me throughout. My guru and great friend the legendary Roger Craver deserves specially glowing mention for his Herculean contribution and support, as do Roy Williams and Laurence Bradbury from Bradbury & Williams. It's nearly 50 years since I first had the privilege of working with Roy and now I wouldn't even contemplate a project like this without them. Jane Fricker was production editor on this book, and was priceless, as so often before. For the illustration on page 37, the Tree of Knowledge, I'm grateful to John Lepp and Jessica Rae Gordon for the idea and the beautiful artwork. I'm happy also to acknowledge the influence and expertise of my colleagues from the old Burnett Associates days, particularly Ernst Goetschi, Karin Weatherup and Jackie Fowler, who I still work with and learn so much from. Also special thanks to Virginia Bushell, for being a superb proof-reader, a rock throughout the later stages of this book, and such fun.

A small number of carefully selected peer reviewers have critiqued the manuscript for this book as it's evolved, pointing out errors and omissions, suggesting improvements and guiding me towards things I should include. I fear my very considerable debt to them will seldom be appreciated, rather I'll get credit for their brilliance and use it to cover up mistakes, with no one any the wiser that really, it's down to them. All the same I'm grateful to Lisa Sargent, David Love, Julie Berthoud-Jury, Tanya Jackson, Karin Weatherup, Alan Clayton, Sean Triner, Ikhlaq Hussain, Nick Allen, Harvey McKinnon, Giles Pegram CBE, Mark Phillips, Ryan Burdock, Michelle Berriman, John Lepp, Andrew Watt, Carlos Miranda and David Carrington. Also to all the SOFII trustees and the hundreds of for-change organisations that I've worked with over five decades. Here I'd like explicitly to acknowledge Nicolette Shaw, Sarah Alexander and all at the National Youth Orchestra of Great Britain, just because their very recent adventure in donor relationship development has been so spectacularly successful and the story of their great achievements in delivering delicious donor experiences hasn't yet been written, hasn't yet been told.

As Scottish people always say whenever they borrow anything of value, 'I will be forever in your debt'. Thank you all.

PERMISSIONS

This page constitutes a continuation of the copyright page.

Other than the very brief quotes that appear throughout this book which, being below 300 words, are generally considered to be 'fair use', the author, wherever possible, has sought permission to quote from copyrighted material or other works by a third party unless that material is obviously in the public domain or its inclusion can also be justified as 'fair use'. More on the author's attitude and approach to quoting from the work of others can be found in the About SOFII page.

Dylan Martinez's photograph of the year on page 22 featuring Patrick Hutchinson and Bryn Male is reproduced by permission of Reuters Pictures.

Exhibit 3
The Treehouse of Knowledge illustration by Jessica Rae Gordon was gifted to SOFII by the Canadian specialist fundraising agency, Agents of Good. With grateful thanks to John Lepp and Jen Love.

Exhibit 5
Photograph courtesy of the Captain Tom Foundation, which was set up subsequent to Captain Tom's record breaking charity walk to ensure his message of hope becomes an enduring legacy.

Exhibit 7
Benjamin Zephaniah's brief comments about the Romans' early attitudes to welfare and African countries' even earlier approach to the same subject come from the BBC TV programme *QI*, series R, Episode 11 – Roaming.

Seneca On Benefits can be found in Wikipedia/ De Beneficiis.

Exhibit 16 and elsewhere
Extracts and quotations from *Thankology: a fundraiser's guide to keeping your donors longer, and giving stronger, through gratitude* are reproduced with the permission of the author, Lisa Sargent.

Exhibit 26
The story of Indra Sinha's adventures in developing long copy advertisements appears with his permission.

Exhibit 31
The photograph of page 124 of a dead goose by Jens Stolt is reproduced by permission of Colourbox.com.

Exhibit 42
The story of Roger Craver's early experiences in political fundraising are published here with his permission.

The majority of other stories and illustrations are taken from the SOFII Foundation's website where most of them have appeared in detail for many years, and so are reproduced here as 'fair use'.